Lucky To Be Alive

A First Expedition to the Himalayas

Lucky To Be Alive

A First Expedition to the Himalayas

By

Angela Benham

nlp

northern liberties press

Philadelphia, Paris,
Kuala Lumpur, London

Published in association with Cheyne Books.

northern liberties press, *An Imprint of Old City Publishing*

Northern Liberties Press
628 North 2nd Street
Philadelphia, PA 19123, USA

Published by:
Old City Publishing, Inc.

Visit our web site at: oldcitypublishing.com

Published in association with Cheyne Books. Dek Palmer Mountaineering Series Editor.

0-9704143-6-6 (paperback)

Library of Congress Cataloging-in-Publication Data

Benham, Angela, 1951-
Lucky to be alive : a first expedition to the Himalayas / Angela Benham.
p. cm.
ISBN 0-9704143-6-6 (pbk.)
1. Benham, Angela, 1951- 2. Mountaineers--Great Britain--Biography.
3. Mountaineering expeditions--Himalaya Mountains. I. Title.
GV199.92.B47 A3 2003
796.52'2'092--dc21

2003006027

*Dedicated to - Brian, David, Max and Susannah
my dear mum Vera and to the Red Rope Tirsuli
North Wall 2001 Expedition Team:
Andrew, Chris D., Chris S., Colin, Roly and Titch*

With Love

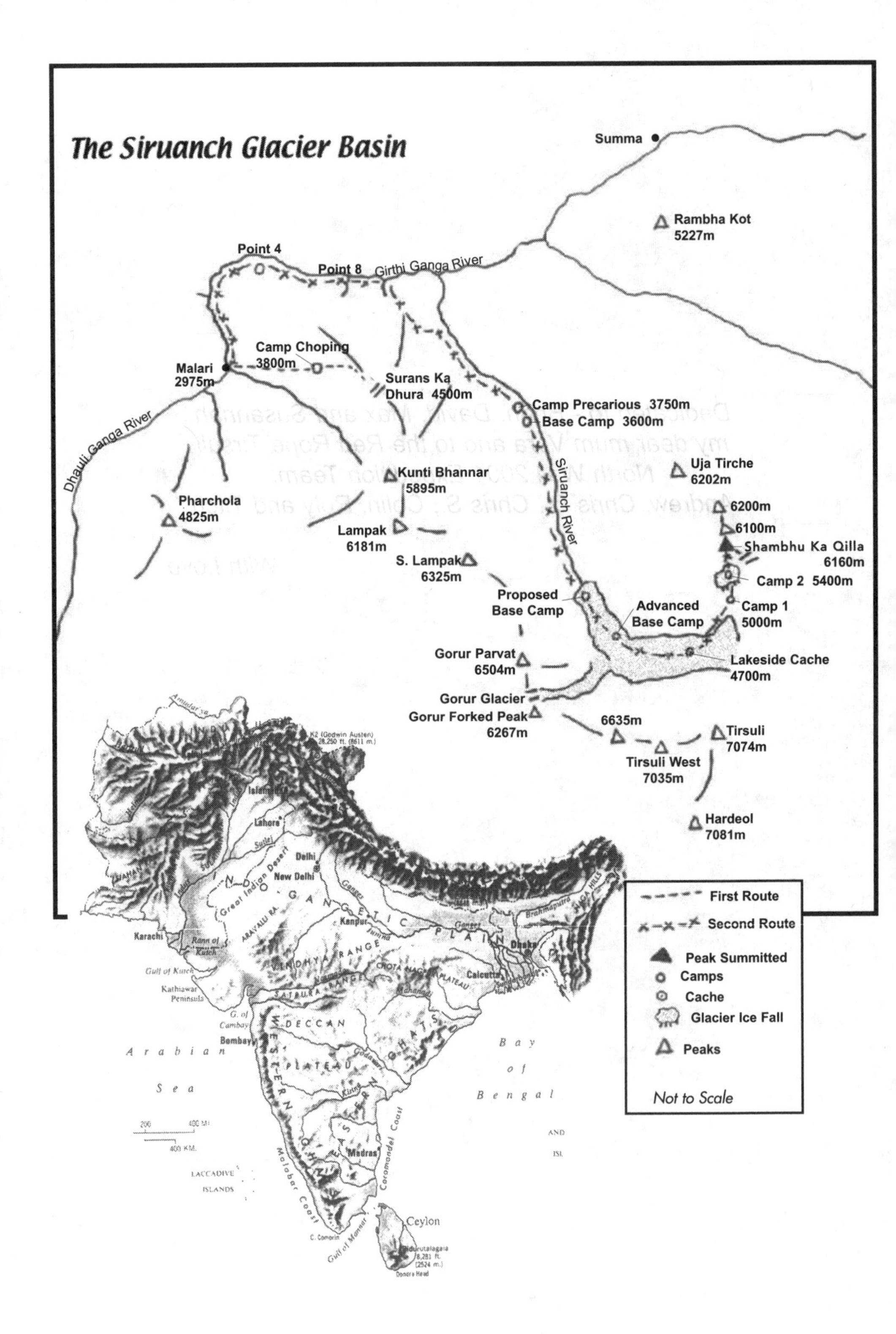
The Siruanch Glacier Basin
Summa
Rambha Kot
5227m
Point 4
Point 8
Girthi Ganga River
Camp Choping
3800m
Malari
2975m
Surans Ka
Dhura 4500m
Camp Precarious 3750m
Base Camp 3600m
Dhauli Ganga River
Siruanch River
Kunti Bhannar
5895m
Uja Tirche
6202m
6200m
6100m
Shambhu Ka Qilla
6160m
Pharchola
4825m
Lampak
6181m
S. Lampak
6325m
Camp 2 5400m
Proposed
Base Camp
Advanced
Base Camp
Camp 1
5000m
Gorur Parvat
6504m
Lakeside Cache
4700m
Gorur Glacier
Gorur Forked Peak
6267m
6635m
Tirsuli
7074m
Tirsuli West
7035m
Hardeol
7081m
First Route
Second Route
Peak Summitted
Camps
Cache
Glacier Ice Fall
Peaks
Not to Scale
K2 (Godwin Austen)
28,250 ft. (8611 m.)
Islamabad
Lahore
Sutlej
Delhi
New Delhi
INDO GANGETIC PLAIN
Great Indian Desert
ARAVALLI RA.
Kanpur
Ganges
Brahmaputra
NAGA HILLS
Dhaka
Karachi
Rann of Kutch
Gulf of Kutch
Kathiawar
Peninsula
VINDHYA RANGE
CHOTA NAGPUR PLATEAU
Calcutta
SATPURA RANGE
G. of
Cambay
Bombay
DECCAN
PLATEAU
WESTERN GHATS
EASTERN GHATS
Arabian
Sea
Bay
of
Bengal
200
400 MI
400 KM.
LACCADIVE
ISLANDS
Madras
Coromandel Coast
Malabar Coast
Ceylon
C. Comorin
Gulf of Mannar
Pidurutalagala
8,281 ft.
(2524 m.)
Dondra Head
AND
ISL

CONTENTS

	Preface	viii
1	Into the Unknown	1
2	A Brown Envelope Drops on the Mat	3
3	"What is Red Rope?"	8
4	To the Alps!	15
5	The Trouble with Maps	19
6	Lists, Permits and Grants	29
7	"Good Luck!"	37
8	Let's Get Packing	42
9	D-Day	45
10	The Road to Malari	53
11	Roly's Dream	65
12	Frustrations Mount	73
13	Follow the Road to Point Eight and Turn Right	81
14	Camp Precarious	88
15	Show me the way to …. the glacier?!	93
16	Race against Time	101
17	All Together for the Final Push	118
18	Summit Day	131
19	The 'Let's Fucking Get Out Of Here' Option	141
20	Shambhu Ka Qilla	147
21	"Are you all in one piece?"	152
22	Because….	158
23	Postscript	162
	Acknowledgements	164

PREFACE

I began writing 'Lucky To be Alive' on 17 July 2001, two months after my return from the Himalayas. By then I had recovered my physical and mental strength after the stresses and strains of the expedition. I wonder if I would ever have thought of writing a book if it hadn't been for Andrew Phillips' comment about submitting an article to the Readers' Digest during our descent of the Siruanch glacier. Thank you, Andrew.

I also question whether I would have managed to finish it without the constant encouragement and enthusiastic support, practical information and advice Chris Smart gave me. She also painstakingly proofread the manuscript. Heartfelt thanks to you, Chris.

Chris wasn't the only person who commented on my first drafts – Vera Benham, Brian Harrison, Cathy Hillman, Titch Kavanagh, Chris and Dick Lewis and Andrew Phillips, all had something encouraging to say. Thanks to you.

Arthur Griffiths has my thanks for the helpful advice he gave me when I came to revise the manuscript. Thank you Arthur.

Thanks to my children – David, Max and Susannah Harrison – who were particularly long-suffering when mum monopolised the computer.

I also wish to thank my friend Ian Robertson from Aberdeen for all the time, training and advice about high altitude climbing and equipment that he gave me. Thank you, Ian.

Thanks also to Tony Whittome of Random House and Peter Hodgkiss of The Ernest Press who wished me good luck with my book.

Penultimate thanks go to Dek Palmer of Cheyne Books for Mountaineers and Ian Mellanby and Guy Griffiths of Northern Liberties Press, for believing my book was worth publishing. Thank you, Ian, Guy and Dek.

But my final and greatest thanks must go to my friends and comrades – Colin Knowles, Chris Drinkwater, Andrew Phillips, Chris Smart, Roly Arnison and Titch Kavanagh – the other six members of the Red Rope Tirsuli North Wall Expedition Team – and to our Indian agent, Vishwas Makhija of India Insight Tours, our Liaison Officer Momoraj Irom and to our India Insight Tours' staff - Norbu Bodh, Ranjit Singh, Yangjor Tshering, Kalu Gurung and Tashi Dorjey – without whom the expedition would not have been possible.

Thank you all. We shared a wonderful experience together.

Angela Benham *September 2002*
Chamonix

O, Death
O, Death
Won't you spare me over til another year
Well, what is this that I can't see
With ice cold hands takin' hold of me
Well, I am death, none can excel
I'll open the door to heaven or hell
Whoa, death someone would pray
Could you wait to call me another day.

Extract from a traditional song from the depression era.
Author Unknown

CHAPTER 1
Into the Unknown

May 16th 2001. The day that could have been my last. I didn't know it as I stood at the bottom of that dark and threatening mountain but oh my, I was full of concerns. The venture was too frightening, too fraught with dangers and risks and fears. What on earth was I doing there?

Despite our uncertainty about the weather the decision was to ascend. Colin, Andrew and I tied onto the rope. As we began to move slowly upwards Chris, Titch and Roly arrived and started to discuss whether to put crampons on straightaway. It soon became clear that crampons were essential and as I balanced awkwardly on the icy slope to put mine on I could see Titch and the others clipping into theirs in the relative comfort of the level glacier.

Our six head torches moved slowly up the South face of the mountain. In places the snow, being deep and wet, was not easy to negotiate. One steep section was covered in ice-covered gravel upon which it was very difficult to get a secure purchase even with crampon points. Colin led the way ahead of us putting in protection where he could. At times I sensed from Andrew's murmurs and sighs that there was a wish that more protection was being used.

Suddenly we came to a halt and Titch, Chris and Roly caught up with us. Colin was momentarily unsure which way to go. We stood for a while and for the first time I became fully aware of the bitterness of the wind cutting into my face. All was dark except the downward sweep of the snow slope beneath my feet. Carefully we began to traverse the slope when there was the long swishing sound of spindrift sliding down from above.

"Oh, my God," I thought. "It's going to avalanche."

Swish, swish – the snow kept coming burying my hand and my ice axe. Nobody moved or said a word. We waited, stood like six pins waiting to be bowled into the void. Then the snow sighed and stopped and I whispered to Andrew, "I'm scared."

"You're committed now," Andrew replied matter-of-factly. "There's no turning back."

"No turning back. No turning back," I thought and knew it was exactly true. There was no arguing with it. I had rejected the option of turning my back on the mountain. Was this a decision that I would regret and rue or worst still be the death of me? I didn't want to die here in the mountains. I wanted to see everybody at home again. My life was good and precious. Why had I chosen to risk it I asked myself? Was it really worth it?

With a sick churning of my stomach I remembered the February morning that fateful brown envelope had appeared on my mat and changed the course of my life.

CHAPTER 2
A Brown Envelope Drops on the Mat

The gloom of those February days. Mornings dark. Daylight hours short and the weather remaining grey and chill. There was heaviness in my steps as I stooped to pick up the post from the mat and flicked through it.

A credit card bill, an appointment card from the optician's, 'The Teacher' magazine (groan – I had loved teaching but now longed for a new career) and a big manila envelope, postmarked Leicester. That's where I live. I turned it over in my hands wondering who had sent it and intrigued, tore it open.

To my astonishment I found a letter inside from the leader of a climbing expedition to the Himalayas. My blood tingled as I read.

> *'Angela – You are invited to apply to join an expedition to climb Tirsuli West, the last unclimbed mountain over 7000 metres (23,000 feet) high in the Kumaon region of the Indian Himalayas.*
>
> *Tirsuli West is in the previously unexplored Upper Siruanch glacier basin and is one of three peaks, Tirsuli West, Tirsuli and Hardeol, known as 'The Trident of Shiva.'*
>
> *The expedition team currently consists of four climbers – Chris Drinkwater (Chris D.), Titch Kavanagh, Colin Knowles and Andrew Phillips. Christine Smart (Chris S.) is a non-climber who will support us at Base Camp. We are currently looking for two more climbers to join our team.*

This was amazing. I'd been invited to apply to join a climbing expedition. For years I'd avidly read books about mountaineering exploits. I'd imagined being frostbitten on Everest, storm-bound on K2, trapped in a crevasse on Siule Grande and had wondered how I would function as the member of a climbing team. Now my unspoken ambition to join an expedition looked like it might be realised. This is why I rushed through to the kitchen, waving the letter in my hand and calling excitedly to my partner:

"Look, here, Brian! I've been invited to apply to join a climbing expedition to the Himalayas!"

"You're not thinking of applying, are you?" was the laconic reply.

"Well...," I paused, sensing a less than enthusiastic response. "I think I might bung an application in. It won't do any harm and I quite like filling in forms. I shouldn't think I'd get accepted."

"Sounds like a waste of time to me."

"Oh, I don't see why..."

I carefully put the brown envelope and papers behind the fruit bowl in the kitchen and got on with domestic tasks.

* * *

The following week was full of activity. I went hill walking in Scotland with a friend I'd made on a winter mountaineering course. There we not only discussed what training would be required for a Himalayan trip but also practised some of the necessary skills in the ice and snow at Glen Doll. I knew that my experience of snow and ice climbing was in fact very limited and I was not too hot on navigation either.

My present interest in climbing and the mountains began in 1992. A work colleague invited me to go along to an indoor climbing wall in Leicester. I jumped at the chance. At that time I had a very stressful teaching job in a special school for children with emotional and behavioural difficulties. It was good to escape into an evening of climbing after a day of striving to deal patiently with children's tantrums and having been family and work orientated for the previous ten years I was ready to concentrate more time on my own personal development. (I had just turned forty after all!).

My first major outdoor climbing trip was to the Lake District. One frenetic June day I left Leicester at 5 a.m., zoomed up to Honister Pass in the Lakes, climbed Gillercombe Buttress, walked out and then drove off to begin the long walk in to scale a classic Lake District climb called Corvus. It was then that I began to perceive the true perversity that is climbing. You spend hours walking in to the start of a route. Your climb to the top seems to fly by and then you've the long walk out again. But at least you have the prospect of a long cool pint of beer waiting for you at the bar – providing you get there before time's called! (Orange juice was the reviving liquor in India).

Later that year I was sat on a ledge on the two thousand foot high Dow Crag belaying my climbing partner (that is holding his rope in a metal belay device that would stop a fall), when it started to snow. I began to feel lonely and my mind in the bleakness of the darkening afternoon began to imagine the worst. What if I couldn't complete the next pitch? What if Mountain Rescue had to be called? Could a helicopter collect me off this tiny ledge? In fact we completed the route with no greater drama than getting lost on the descent but as you can see I'm not the most confident or cocky of climbers. A sense of foreboding is more my trait.

Little did I think then that I would take myself to the back of beyond where there are no Mountain Rescue Services.

Over the following years I sought to build up my climbing experience as much as I could without neglecting my family or my job. I was not going to achieve brilliantly high climbing grades (damn it!) but I enjoyed the challenge to improve.

I went on climbing courses with different organisations. I enjoyed learning new skills in good company and surrounded by beautiful countryside but was forever feeling that my two steps forward, were followed by one step back, because I couldn't find the opportunities to consolidate my climbing skills. Then in 1995 I contacted members of the socialist walking and climbing club Red Rope, attracted by its non-sexist, non-racist, non-elitist stance, and began climbing with them.

It's been said that people either love or loathe climbing. My partner has, in fact, exclaimed with some bitterness that I'm obsessed with it. In part it's true of course. That's why when I returned from my Scottish jaunt I took the brown envelope down from behind the fruit bowl and retired to the dining room table to fill in the application form. I knew it would cause conflict. But there was part of me that thought, "It's only an academic exercise. Nothing will come of it." And there was another part of me that hoped with trepidation that something would.

First of all there was the Climbing Experience sheet to complete with examples of significant climbs and mountaineering routes I'd done. I was pleased that I could write that I had trekking experience in the Annapurna region of Nepal even though it had been twenty-two years earlier when I returned from teaching with Voluntary Service Overseas in Thailand. The highest mountain I had climbed was the 3163 metre (10,377 foot) Cima di Mezzo of Monte Cristallo in the Dolomites in Italy. The route has 'vie ferrate', metal cableways and ladders set into the mountain that you can clip onto with a karabiner (a metal link with a safety closure) as a means of protection.

I included more recent examples of my mountaineering in Scotland and North Wales. In clammy thick mist I had climbed ten Munros – mountains over three thousand feet high – in the Black Cuillin in Skye without seeing a single view.

Having completed my climbing experience details I had to write a letter citing a member of the climbing team as a referee.

I'd climbed with the expedition leader, Colin Knowles, so I chose him and wrote:

> *Colin is familiar with my weaknesses and strengths as a climber. He knows I'm not a bold leader although I have successfully led a number of single and multi-pitch Very Severe grade climbs. I am a steady second with stamina and enthusiasm.*

I'm a late starter who has tried to get as much mountaineering experience as possible while having to take account of raising a family of three kids. I took heart from Julie Tullis when I read her book 'Clouds from Both Sides' and realised she was in her forties when she became a mountaineer.

I am also well aware that my actual snow and ice experience is not vast. I imagine that the team will be looking for climbers who are both confident, skilled rock, snow and ice climbers and clear thinking navigators for such a serious undertaking as a 23,000 foot peak. Consequently I think it's unlikely that you'll consider me as suitable for an assault on the summit.

However if the team were looking for an easy-going individual who can climb and carry loads and who'd be willing to commit time and hard work to the success of the expedition that would be me. Indeed having read so much about climbing expeditions over the last seven years or so I would happily help with the organisation in the UK without the trip to India if that was what circumstances demanded.

I re-read the letter, concluded 'All best wishes for the task ahead', signed my name and took it in to show Brian who was watching some Sunday evening television. He read it without smiling.

"So you're going ahead then?"

"Well, yes, I can't see it'll do any harm."

"What you've said is right. You haven't got enough experience.... and six weeks is a long time. You know high altitude climbing's suicide."

"I don't know what you're worried about?" I replied. "I doubt that I'll get accepted and if I am, I expect I'll stay at Base Camp. Not everybody dies anyway." I paused and then continued. "I'm going to send it anyway. I've written it now."

I left the room and next day my white envelope dropped into the post box.

CHAPTER 3
What is Red Rope?

As I grunted and huffed and puffed with my right leg stuck behind the awkward rock bulge I felt relieved Melanie had led this pitch on Bezel, a route in North Wales.

"Having a bit of bother, Mel," I shouted and started berating myself as I strained once again to make the move.

"Go on, Angela. You can't hang around here all day." I didn't. I fell off for the second time and banged my knee. Four-letter words seared the sky. I think being a repressed evangelical Christian during my teenage years has encouraged me to become an extremely foul-mouthed climber at moments of stress. All the previously swallowed curses and rages erupt with the feelings of frustration and fear.

"What the fucking hell are you doing, you stupid shit?" I muttered to myself through clenched teeth. "You've got to bloody well pull!"

So I pulled, and I pulled hard. "And use your bloody feet to push." Yes, that was good advice I was giving myself now. I pulled and pushed and finally moved upwards, leaving bits of skin stuck to the rock. Stren…u….ous.

"Made it, at last," I said when I reached Mel on her belay ledge. It had been a satisfying climb despite (or because of) the difficulties. One of many that I've done with members of the Red Rope Socialist Mountaineering and Rambling Club.

I was prompted to join this small national club after some months of feeling I was excluded from trips with my local club because I was the only woman. I knew that Leicester Red Rope had a number of female members and although loath to label myself politically I knew I was in sympathy with the club's egalitarian ideals. On my first climbing trip with the Club we went to a grit stone crag in the Peak District National Park. I led some easy routes and seconded a more testing one, which a short time afterwards, was breezily soloed by a passing climber. Such a difference in class, I thought wistfully, as I watched him climb without the security of a rope. But, if he could do that, surely I could lead 'Twenty foot crack,' an easier climb. I did, but whereas he floated effortlessly up the much harder climb I scrabbled with as much elegance and poise as a walrus. Nonetheless this was progress for me. I still recalled with some unease the remarks that I had overheard one male climber make about women being dragged up climbs. I wanted to be a good, skilled climber in my own right if my character, psychology and ability were up to it.

It was three months later that I heard the radio news announce the loss of Alison Hargreaves on the descent from the second highest mountain in the world, K2. She was a world-renowned climber whose ability, character and psychology, as far as I could glean it from newspaper reports, I respected.

I'd read her account of her solo ascent of the Croz Spur in the Alps in High, the climbing magazine. It included six photographs of her as a tiny dot of humanity powering her way determinedly up the vast North Face of the Grandes Jorasses. At one point the ice shattered, taking her left foothold with it. She was left suspended from two delicate axe placements – spindrift flowing so thickly she feared it would wash her away.

'Panic didn't seem appropriate.' She wrote in her article 'I kicked another placement in the tiny bit of ice remaining and closing my eyes I pulled on up and gently taking one of the axes out of the ice reached out for another placement. That felt firm.'

I found it hard to imagine that I could ever have the boldness and independence of spirit to attempt such an enterprise on my own. This frustrated me because it was that superlative degree of competence that I really wanted to attain. No way could I see myself having the guts to do a big mountain route alone but part of me desperately wished that I had.

Joe Simpson reports in his book 'Dark Shadows Falling' that Alison Hargreaves' response to a question asking her why she took the extra risks of soloing was that she actually considered it safer to go alone. 'If there is no one else to lean on, you have to get on with it, do the sensible thing and neglect nothing, because you know your life depends on it.' I understood what she meant by that.

One January I was alone in the Cairngorm Mountains. The mist drifted in thickly at times and there was deep snow underfoot. Few people were out on the hills. I wasn't happy about the conditions and became acutely aware that it was solely up to me to decide which route to take. It certainly concentrated my mind and after a couple of errors I felt relieved when it became clear that I was heading in the right direction for a nice cup of tea. But I suffered distinct feelings of vulnerability, which weren't pleasant. How do you conquer these? Perhaps the answer is to face the beast and commit yourself to these testing situations more frequently. This would build up practical strategies and skills on the hills and boost your confidence in yourself. That's the theory. Part of the difficulty in putting it into practice is the general whiff of social opprobrium that can still be afforded women who are considered to wantonly court risk. "Well, what did she expect, she was asking for it." "Why wasn't she at home being a mother to her children?"

I've discussed my ambivalence with other climbers. Climbing with Colin one day I bemoaned the fact that men seemed to be able to lead climbs so much more easily than me. Colin wondered if biology did play a part; in so far as the female of the human species generally takes a primary role in raising the young and is consequently more inclined to avoid danger for the sake of the offspring than the male. It's certainly true that I wouldn't have applied for the expedition if I hadn't believed that my children were mature enough to survive the trauma of their mother's death in the mountains without deep psychological damage. For unlike Alison Hargreaves, climbing is not my job. It 's a hobby adopted in later life although it does fulfil a therapeutic and self-discovery role, too.

The majority of hard, committed climbers tend to be younger men without family responsibilities. When babies arrive on the scene things may change. Bold climbers who become fathers can learn to enjoy less challenging climbs. It must be that each individual has to examine their situation and come to their own decision about what risks they are willing to take. How can anyone else decide for them? In the June 1998 issue of Climber magazine Ed Douglas quotes from a 1994 interview given by Alison Hargreaves. In it she said that 'Everybody takes risks in whatever they do.... I have weighed the risks and I believe they are worth taking." Tragically Alison Hargreaves' luck ran out. She died on K2 and her children were left without a mother. What luck would I have in the Himalayas?

The fear that I might die in the mountains was without doubt a major concern of my partner's. One of the first remarks Brian made after I told him I'd been accepted as a climbing member of the Tirsuli North Wall Expedition 2001 team was, "You're assuming that I'll look after the children?"

"What do you mean I'm assuming you'll look after the children?" I responded surprised at the comment.

"You will, won't you? You're their father as much as I'm their mother." I thought but did not say. I recalled the weeks that I had looked after David, Max and Susannah when they were little and Brian was overseas on exotic working holidays. This didn't bode well.

Brian replied, "Six weeks is a long time."

"Yes, it is but David will be at University and Max will be seventeen and Susie will be fourteen. They're not babies anymore."

No more was said then.

In fact all was quiet on the Tirsuli front until Brian returned from a trip to France and announced that he wanted to have a talk. We sat down at the pine table in the kitchen and with a stern face Brian said he'd been talking to his French friend about the expedition and felt I ought to reconsider my decision to go.

"Why?" I replied slowly.

"You know, Himalayan climbing's incredibly dangerous. How many of these high altitude climbers get killed? The odds are stacked against you. There's the danger of avalanches, frostbite, altitude sickness. And you haven't got enough experience."

Brian looked at me squarely and I felt a chill in my heart.

"I know I haven't got a great deal of experience," I agreed, "but I'm working on that. I've got a year to train. I've already started. As for getting killed, I'm hoping not to get killed. You know I could just as easily get killed here. I could get knocked down by a bus tomorrow, couldn't I?"

I looked at Brian, feeling the tension in the air.

"That's much less likely than you dying from altitude sickness."

"But all these years I've been reading about expeditions and here's my chance to go on one. I want to go."

"They've only accepted you because they need the money." Brian countered.

I blenched at this remark. I knew the people involved and this couldn't be the case.

"I don't think so, Brian." I said coldly.

Angered and frustrated by my stubbornness Brian stood up from the table and retorted, "You're just being foolhardy. And you're too old!"

A heavy smouldering cloud enveloped the whole kitchen. I was consumed with icy rage. Foolhardy. Too old. He can't stop me going. The kids had given me their blessing. "Go for it," Susannah had said. My mum was worried sick but accepted that it was important to me. "You always do what you want anyway, whatever I say. Just be careful!"

I was going. If it meant the most drastic action, I was going. This was my fiftieth year and this was my birthday present to myself even if it meant my death.

"I am going, Brian." I said.

The next few days were not easy. Communications between Brian and myself broke down completely. At the same time I learnt that it was going to be difficult getting the required six weeks' leave from my teaching post despite the encouraging response from my head teacher.

Yet I knew deep down that I wanted this adventure even if it meant resigning my job.

Brian came to recognise the strength of my resolution too. A woman ski guide acquaintance with Himalayan climbing experience had reassured him that it was a matter of fitness and attitude rather than age that would affect a person's performance at altitude. She'd also recommended that our climbing team should take a portable altitude bag to treat any case of severe altitude sickness. One evening Brian asked if our team would be taking an altitude bag. I said that decisions about equipment would be made in September when the full team met but I'd certainly suggest that we should.

Brian continued. "I also think that if you're going to the Himalayas, you need to get yourself to the Alps and do some training there."

I blinked.

"Would that be okay with you?"

"Well, yes. If you're going, it's important you know what you're doing."

I felt a surge of relief and warmth sweep over me. This was a truce.

"That's great." I said with a smile. "I'll arrange to do an Alpine Mountaineering course. Thanks, Brian."

"Just don't get killed, that's all I ask," Brian added.

"I don't plan to." I laughed and we finished off a bottle of wine.

It's with a sense of irony, considering what happened in

the Himalayas, that I recall the inscription my long-suffering partner wrote in a climbing book he gave me one Christmas.

To Angela
With much love from Brian
(and don't break your neck – you're irreplaceable!)

So what is Red Rope? It's a democratic socialist walking and climbing club, which aims to give individuals, whatever their background, the opportunity to develop their mountaineering skills and in some cases to achieve their ambition.

During my first climbing outing after our return from the Himalayas I asked Titch how it happened that I was offered a place on the expedition when my actual mountaineering experience was small. His reply was, "That's Red Rope."

CHAPTER 4
To the Alps!

It was good fortune that I'd already arranged a number of climbing trips for the year 2000 which would contribute to what now had to be a rigorous training programme in preparation for the Himalayas.

Even before my place on the expedition was confirmed I'd practised my abseiling technique on a beautiful cliff called Cabezon d'Oro in Spain. Abseiling is the use of a doubled rope and metal device to descend a mountain as quickly and as safely as possible. It's an essential but notoriously dangerous aspect of mountaineering due to anchors failing and climber error. It was the first time I'd done multiple abseils down a crag and involved climbing across a knife-edged rocky ridge to a metal abseil ring at the top of the cliff. There I had to loop the climbing rope through the ring, clip onto the rope with my abseil device and safety prusik knot and slide down the rope to the next abseil point. As I concentrated on the procedure I was surrounded by the rich aromatic scent of thyme and rosemary shrubs and warm sunlight shimmering through the bushes. How different the environment would be in the Himalayan Mountains.

I was accepted as a climber on the Red Rope Tirsuli North Wall expedition team the day after I'd committed myself to a climbing trip on the island of Lundy in the Bristol Channel. I'd have to miss the team's first meeting.

"Good training climbing there," Colin reassured me.

Naturalists as well as alpinists gravitate towards Lundy, which is a haven for rare flora and fauna as well as climbers in pursuit of spectacular sea-cliff climbing. My first climb was up a rock pinnacle while three friends attempted a more difficult crack climb. Sat on top of my granite tower I noticed a bearded man waving his arms and shouting at my friends. What had they done?

Without realising it they'd pulled up some rare Lundy Cabbage plants which grow naturally nowhere else in the world and are counted annually by scientists such as this angry man. Here was a horrible failure in our reading of the Lundy Climbing Guide, which is thoroughly researched so as to prevent climbers damaging the environment in which they love to climb.

Chastened, we confirmed in the Guide that the sea-cliffs on the west coast of the island where we'd find 'The Devil's Slide', the classic Lundy climb, weren't restricted because of breeding seabirds. The first stage of the route is a 165 foot abseil to a sea-splashed ledge at the foot of this massive slab of black and orange streaked granite, sweeping satanically down into the Atlantic Ocean. I led the first two pitches run into one. My friend led the third. It was delicate slab climbing in a magnificent position below the azure sky above the azure sea. Unfortunately this factor was not appreciated by a disgruntled seagull, which took umbrage at our presence and began dive-bombing me on the airy traverse of pitch four.

What do you do when images from Hitchcock's film 'The Birds' flash through your mind as you are tiptoeing daintily leftwards two hundred feet above the foaming sea? You keep your head down and alternate between attempting to pacify the enraged feathered fury by soothingly calling, "It's okay, seagull, I'm not going to hurt you." and desperately trying to intimidate it by screaming at the top of your voice, "Fuck off, you stupid lunatic bird!" Arriving at the finish of the route with both eyes and all limbs intact convinced me that this strategy had worked. It was a memorable climb and good training for stress management.

Once back from Lundy I began to make enquiries about suitable snow and ice climbing courses in Switzerland, keen to follow my husband's injunction, "Get thee to the Alps!" A friend recommended the well-respected British climber Martin Moran's Introductory Alpine Course so I plumped for that. As always I checked my will and funeral wishes were in order before I left and as a sop to my conscience decorated my daughter's bedroom.

Whereas Himalayan mountaineering usually involves establishing a series of camps up the mountainside over a number of weeks with a well-equipped Base Camp at the bottom and climbers moving up and down between the camps stashing gear and food, climbing in the Alps often involves walking to a mountain hut with beds, food and drinks one day and making an assault on the mountain early the following morning.

The route to the Dix Mountain Hut in the Valais Alps led us up steep grassy slopes above the village of Arolla and through a rising rocky landscape to a precipitous drop – the Pas de Chevres. There the guides belayed us down iron ladders onto the dry Cheilon glacier below, which had to be crossed to reach the hut on the other side. Dry glaciers are less dangerous than wet glaciers because crevasses are usually visible. Midway across the glacial moraine it poured with rain and to my surprise the English guide produced an umbrella from his sack, put it up and proceeded to battle against the fierce alpine storm. Alas, one gust was too strong and the umbrella snapped. I slept badly that night worried our climb would be cancelled because of the weather and my training disrupted.

But it wasn't. It was a beautiful clear cold alpine dawn and with crampons on we moved up what was now an ice-covered glacier. Difficulties arose when we found that the normally benign snow slope was covered with potentially treacherous ice and a bitterly cold wind chilled us to the bone on the exposed terrain.

Suddenly one of the guides took my ice axe and used it to

bash his axe into the ice for a belay. He brusquely told us to kick out platforms for our feet on the slope and then moved swiftly up the ice. A call to climb came and we were relieved to be on the move again. On the second steeper pitch the guide used an ice screw, which he left for me to take out.

"Climb!" came the shout and I tried to remove the first ice screw of my life.

"Which way do you turn the bloody thing?" I muttered to myself, " and why won't it bloody well budge?"

The screw was so stiff to turn with my fingers that I broke into a sweat getting it out. I learnt later that the guide had used his ice axe pick to tighten the screw and that I should have used mine to loosen it. Another lesson learnt.

We had reached the 3785 metre (12,415 foot) false summit of Mont Blanc de Cheilon. The previous night's weather conditions had made it unsafe to attempt the ridge to the true summit but we had a marvellous view of Whymper's Matterhorn from our position. As we made our descent down rolling snowy slopes, now sheltered from wind-chill, I felt sure that the Himalayas were for me, little thinking that confronted with the reality of the challenge I would come to question my sanity at being there.

CHAPTER 5
The Trouble with Maps

There is a pile of Ordnance Survey maps on my bedroom bookshelf. Some are tatty around the edges and the Kinder Scout plateau is all but worn away on my Peak District National Park map. Nonetheless I regard them as dependable navigation instruments. There's the possibility a stream may have disappeared underground or some forestry may have been felled but when a hill is marked, I expect there to be a hill, and if it's not visible, it's due to a navigational error on my part rather than a failing in the map. Maps of remote, little explored areas of the world are much less reliable. It was this sense of venturing into the unknown that made our expedition doubly exciting. We weren't following the tracks of a legion of other adventurers. We were aiming to step where nobody had stepped before.

When the team looked at the relevant section of the map at our first meeting we saw the north face of the seven thousand and thirty five metre (23,081 foot) mountain Tirsuli West rising above the unexplored Upper Siruanch glacier basin. We were to discover that this glacier basin was a long and arduous trek from the nearest settlement, the small road head village of Malari. Earlier explorers had concentrated their attention on mountain peaks at the road end of the valley. In 1937 Uja Tirche (6202m, 20,347ft) was climbed via the West-South-West ridge. Thirteen years later four Scotsmen – W.H. Murray, Tom Weir, Douglas Scott and Tom

MacKinnon – climbed the same mountain via the North Ridge. W.H. Murray described his view of the north wall of Tirsuli rising up at the back of the Siruanch glacier running seven miles southwards, 'fed by a vast horseshoe of ten 20,000-foot mountains'.

'Probably we were the first mountaineers ever to see that stupendous face – a precipice of snow and ice three miles long.'

It was the colour picture of Tirsuli in Murray's book 'The Scottish Himalayan Expedition' which initially aroused, our expedition leader, Colin's interest in the unclimbed north wall of Tirsuli West.

In 1984 Ajit Shelat and Chandrashekhar Tambat set out to do an ascent of Uja Tirche. They climbed up the steep hill-side to the east of Malari en route for the Surans ka Dhura pass (c4500m / 14,764ft) and the following day descended to the Chilkuanch camping ground (3600m,11,811ft) fifty metres above the Siruanch river. Our expedition thought that this was the most likely route we'd follow into the Siruanch glacier.

In the same year as Shelat and Tambat summitted Uja Tirche, Harish Kapadia was exploring the eastern approach to the Siruanch glacier basin. His small trekking party wanted to look at Chalab (6160m / 20,210ft) and Kholi (6114m / 20,059ft). However having climbed high up the North Ridge of Chalab the group decided that it wasn't well enough equipped to proceed and turned back. Our team was to adopt Chalab as our summit objective if Tirsuli West proved impossible, although a surprise was in store.

The first attempt to climb Tirsuli ended in tragedy when an avalanche struck four members of the Polish expedition team and it wasn't until 1966 that Chancal Mitra's team finally conquered the mountain.

Tirsuli West remained unclimbed.

In 1995 Roger Payne and Julie-Ann Clyma attempted a lightweight ascent of the mountain from the Bagini Barak side. They had to turn back, defeated by the looseness and unpredictability of the rock.

The aim of our 2001 team was to redress the balance by

reconnoitring the northern approach to Tirsuli West and the Tirsuli North Wall. I knew Colin, the leader, and his partner Chris Smart quite well because we were members of Leicester Red Rope. I'd met three of the other team members briefly at a Red Rope weekend in North Wales in 1998. Chris Drinkwater saved my day's climbing by finding my lost car keys nestling in the campsite grass. Titch, I remembered being a big hairy man with young children and Andrew I could picture eating bacon sandwiches in the mess tent. Roly Arnison, the youngest team member, was new to all of us except Titch who had been his referee. The team was complete by the 12th March 2000 but it was autumn before we all met together for the first time. Colin had chosen to have a six strong climbing party because smaller parties are vulnerable to illness, injury and acute mountain sickness. Larger ones are prone to suffer poor inter-personal relationships and fragmentation. The belief was a party of six would give a fair chance of the team achieving its objective. Four of the team members had completed a successful Himalayan expedition in 1997 to CB11, a six thousand metre (19,685 foot) virgin peak in the Lahaul region of northern India. Colin, Titch and Andrew had been the climbers. Chris Smart (Chris S.) had provided support at Base Camp.

When Colin told me that I had been accepted on the expedition as a climber he made a point of mentioning gender issues. On the actual climb I would be the only female amidst five males. I said that I didn't think that this would cause any major difficulties. It's commonplace in mountaineering activities for men and women to bunk down together and I felt quite relaxed about sharing a tent with any of the fellas. Later in the year at one of the team's training session chats over chip butties (French fry sandwiches) Colin introduced a discussion about climbing partners and sleeping partners on the expedition. I explained that I thought it could become onerous if climbing partnerships were set so that one team member was destined to partner me for the whole trip. Being the least experienced and least confident climber I foresaw this putting extra pressure on the climber partnering me. Colin reprimanded me for putting myself down but I felt I was assessing my skills and the possible strains realistically. I suggested that it would be best if I were shared around. "I'd like the chance to sleep and climb with everybody." I said. (As it happened the only person I never slept with was the other woman, Chris Smart).

What I interpreted as an unconscious psychological strategy for coping with authority and role issues amongst the team was the revival of Chris and Colin's nicknames from their 1997 Himalayan expedition. They would at various times be referred to as Mum and Dad (though not by me). Meanwhile I was de-sexed by becoming Aunty Ange. Both Chris Drinkwater and Roly are very tall slim men, aged 49 and 31 respectively. They were the thin boys, whereas Titch and Andrew, the stockier pair aged 37 and 39 respectively, were the fat boys. Harmonious inter-personal relationships on a mentally and physically demanding expedition are extremely important. Inevitably a few minor tensions did arise during the course of the trip but my view is that the regular meetings and sharing of individual's views, ideas, feelings and opinions helped ensure that any negative sentiments were soon assuaged. Furthermore, Colin as a leader seemed ever sensitive to each team member's individual psyche and made determined efforts to maintain its good health.

It was during a team meeting at Camp Choping above Malari that Colin raised the question of having an official team deputy leader in case he was out of action for some reason. (There had been an earlier instance in Malari when Colin, struck down by a bug, had asked Titch and Andrew to conduct discussions with Raju, the head porter, about the best route into the Siruanch glacier). The team was asked its views on the matter. I said that we'd appreciated the direction of a leader when Chris Drinkwater had mysteriously gone missing at the end of our day's acclimatisation walk into the hills surrounding Malari.

Colin, Chris Smart and I were on our way back to Malari along the steep hillside track. The four boys – Titch, Roly, Andrew and Chris D. – had forged on ahead in the morning and had not been seen since. All of a sudden there was a shout and looking up to the ridge above I saw some figures waving their walking poles at me. "Good," I thought, "That's where they are." The fellows bounded down the hillside and we gathered in a group where there were some derelict stone water tanks and walls. Having excitedly exchanged news about our various discoveries it suddenly dawned upon us that Chris Drinkwater had not arrived. Where was he?

I thought I'd seen four people wave at me from the ridge. Titch raced back up to see if Chris D. had been delayed there somehow. Colin, accompanied by Roly, went back along the forest path that we'd used. Andrew and I continued along the hillside path to see if we could catch sight of a purple-fleeced Chris there. He seemed to have disappeared into thin air. We continued searching and calling for about forty-five minutes to no avail. There was a sense of anxiety and uncertainty about what to do next until Colin called us together and gave his assessment of the situation. We'd spent time trying to locate Chris. Now we could continue to Malari hoping to meet up with him on the way. If we didn't the porters gathering there would be much quicker and more efficient at effecting a search in the area than us. What did we think? We agreed this made good sense and pressed on down the hillside. Within half an hour Chris was spotted fighting his way through the undergrowth far below the true path. The relieved shout, "What you doing down there, Chris?" echoed across the green slopes to the river gorge below.

Without doubt even a small team of seven benefited from individual members having leadership responsibilities.

"I propose Titch," said Andrew at Camp Choping.

"I second that," I added.

"Okay by you, Titch?" Colin checked and then, after a pause continued, "And I was wondering, Andrew, if you'd be interested in playing a part, too?"

Everybody agreed. So Titch and Andrew became our joint deputy leaders. Both were experienced mountaineers who'd been with Colin on the Red Rope expedition in 1997. It was appropriate that both should have leadership roles and Colin displayed his ability to achieve that diplomatically and democratically.

Feeling mellow towards the end of the expedition Andrew began suggesting animal names that he considered matched the different team members' characteristics.

"How about Colin as a badger?" he suggested.

"A badger – why a badger?" I said, wondering if Andrew was thinking of Colin's thick black beard.

"Well, aren't badgers meant to be wise?" Andrew continued.

"Wise and carriers of T.B." I could have said.

Titch, Andrew and I were sat by the lone tree at the top of the gruelling five hundred metre (1,640 foot) climb through the rhododendron bushes en route for the Siruanch glacier for the last time. We were waiting for Chris Drinkwater and Roly who had been delayed by calls of nature, whiling away the time looking down on the tiny green tents at Base Camp and playing this daft naming game. Andrew named himself a camel.

"Why a camel?" I queried again.

"Well, I'm grumpy and I'm always getting the hump," Andrew replied. Titch and I both looked at each other and laughed, not inclined to disagree.

I was not so happy when Andrew went on to suggest that I was a hedgehog because I was a bit prickly and had a penchant for rolling down hills (more of that later).

"I'm only prickly with you!" I protested loudly.

Of course there was a grain of truth in what Andrew said. What I considered my generally conciliatory and patient air had a number of times been ruffled by what I categorised as Andrew's moaning.

"Oh, shut up, Andrew," I'd hear myself saying.

As for Titch, being Titch the Yak – that seemed perfectly apt. Titch was strong and solid, the speediest and steadiest walker of us all despite his big frame. He was dependable and of the sweetest disposition even though he teased me relentlessly about my bad hair days and was an incorrigible joker. There was the case of the missing stoves!

* * *

Having arrived at our Delhi hotel in the early hours of the morning after a seven-hour plane flight from Zurich and little sleep the previous night we were not at our best. The bags containing our personal gear and our communal equipment were shoved into cupboards and corners in our different hotel rooms. A couple of days later when we were meeting to prepare for the two day bus journey up north to Joshimath Colin casually enquired, "Where are the stoves?" Colin had spent a considerable amount of time and effort making and trialling these three hanging aluminium gas stoves. It would be a disaster if they'd been left on the aeroplane or forgotten on the airport bus. We looked at each other. "Where are the stoves?" was a good question. We didn't know. We'd have to check through the sacks of communal gear. We did count the sacks when we got to the hotel, didn't we?

The team dispersed to their rooms and began their rummagings. Colin phoned to say he'd searched the sacks in his room and there were no stoves. Meanwhile, Titch, who was sharing a room with Chris Drinkwater and me, uncovered the somewhat crushed but recognisable stoves at the bottom of one of the sacks in our cupboards. Off he went to Andrew and Roly's room, not to share the good news but to spin out the agony as long as he could, claiming that the stoves could not be found anywhere. I marvelled at his wickedness. Roly was far from amused when the truth finally emerged and it wasn't the first time that he was heard to groan in some anguish, "Not another joke, Titch, noooooooooo….!" (Not that Roly was beyond a joke or two!). He and Titch were in fact good mates. After spending several days cooped up in a high altitude tent together the pair of them amused themselves by adding 'Do not piss in the tent' to the list of 'Do nots' on the tent manufacturer's label. I was to discover that drinking water and passing water were frequent topics of conversation on high altitude expeditions.

Roly, a slim man, was also extremely tall and gangly. I got rather a reputation for gullibility because one Delhi day when we were swimming in the hotel pool I asked Roly how tall he was. " I'm eight foot six inches," he joked. I replied in all seriousness, "Gosh! I didn't realise you were that tall!" But then, I never was a one for figures. I've a photo of Roly looking like a nineteenth century explorer – arms folded in shorts with knobbly knees and a safari-like hat. He was nicknamed the Giraffe as he came ambling with long strides up the slope. Roly was gentle, thoughtful, calm and thorough. That was a good thing too because he was our medical officer and he had a number of medical incidents to deal with during our six weeks away.

Roly had left behind Hannah, his three month old baby and Jana, his partner. Jana circulated a photograph she'd called 'Excess Baggage' just before our departure, which showed Hannah fast asleep in her car seat, surrounded by our bags of gear.

All the team had family and loved ones who were inevitably affected by the members' decision to set off on a potentially dangerous adventure. Titch's two young girls had painted his toenails so throughout the trip the pink and purple gloss was there as a reminder of them. He'd left the girls a pre-recorded tape of funny stories. We all knew there were risks but once you're born you are faced with the inevitable risk of dying and we held fast to the expedition statement:

> *This trip is as much about meeting other people and cultures as it is about climbing a mountain. Our imperative is that everyone comes back alive. Our aim is that we enjoy our time together.*

Finally there were two Chrises in our team, Christine, known as Chris Smart (Chris S.), our Base Camp support, and Chris Drinkwater (Chris D.). "The best ice-climber amongst us." as Colin said on summit day. Chris Smart played a vital role in many ways but one, which the team appreciated particularly, was her sensitive tendering of the beer kit brew while we were up the mountain. She had the unenviable task of waiting a whole week at Base Camp, watching and wondering about our progress on the mountain as grim weather enveloped the peaks.

As for Chris Drinkwater, our second thin man, he was tall, bespectacled and stately. Before the team set off to India he'd sported a long full bushy beard and despite shaving it off Chris retained a meditative, prophet-like air. Indeed he had, as we were to discover from his passport, a doctorate although not precisely in philosophy. Andrew regarded Chris D. and I as being the quiet ones and we ended up sharing a hotel room more often than not. One of the reasons why Chris was quiet and tended to be on the periphery of conversations and kerfuffle was that he was hard of hearing and a hesitant speaker. He felt much more comfortable interacting in one-to-one situations. I felt a little unsure about the suggested animal designated to Chris. Was it Chris the Sloth as he stepped carefully and unhurriedly through the tangle of branches and twigs and leaves on the rhododendron slope?

I assumed that Andrew was referring to Chris D. almost invariably being the last member of the team to have got his gear sorted and ready for departure. Chris was aware of his tendency to faff at times and sought people's understanding as he strove to be more organised. The team was generally tolerant of each other's little foibles but an irritable comment would occasionally slip out. I felt very warmly towards Andrew but he exasperated me sometimes because of his tendency to 'wear his heart on his sleeve' and just blurt things out. I interpreted this as whingeing and self-centredness.

"For goodness sake, Andrew," I'd say, "Were you an only child?"

Likewise you might hear one of the team waiting to set off up or down the glacier mutter.

"Where's Chris Drinkwater? Don't tell me. He's sorting his gear."

And of course, I aggravated others too. The day after we returned from the summit it was necessary to fix some ropes across a rushing river which had been frozen solid on our journey into Base Camp at the very start of the Himalayan spring. Colin asked for volunteers to help him with this job. Despite having no experience of fixing rope I agreed to go as no one else volunteered. While Colin was showing me how to hammer in a piton (a metal peg) I called myself stupid because I didn't hit it right.

"I'd be happy if you'd stop calling yourself stupid," Colin exclaimed crossly.

I was taken aback and didn't know what to say. I tried to understand what Colin meant by his outburst. I knew I wasn't really stupid but I did feel impatient with myself when I couldn't master tasks as well as I would like to. A little later on, Colin apologised for being grumpy, adding, "How can you expect yourself to get it right first time, you've never done it before, Ange. It's a matter of building up on previous knowledge and experience. Stop being so hard on yourself."

The trouble was I wanted to be the best piton-placer in the whole wide world!

CHAPTER 6
Lists, Permits and Grants

Okay, it might mean I'm anal-retentive and need to maintain control but I do adore lists – shopping lists, gear lists, job lists, book lists, film credit lists, name lists, packing lists, any lists. The Tirsuli North Wall expedition wasn't to deny my craving because from March 2000 to April 2001 my computer system was bombarded with all manner of lists and communications. What's more I myself could contribute to the list of lists.

One of the first I received via e-mail was five pages long and detailed the personal and collective gear we might require for the expedition. As I ran my eyes down it I noted that I wouldn't need shaving gear though sanitary towels might come in handy. I was undecided about the pee bottle. A pillow and camping seat kit were luxuries that I could forego. I'd only a vague idea what avalanche transceivers and solar chargers were for and wondered what kind of man a leatherman was. Later on I was intrigued to hear that Roly was given one for Christmas (having hidden my ignorance) and then disappointed to discover that all it was, was a fancy toolkit.

This personal and collective gear list was the team's focus of attention for its first full meeting in September 2000. All seven of us congregated with our bulging boxes and bags of gear at a church hall in Leicester. The objective of the meeting was to consider our equipment's suitability for the task, to weigh it and to begin to identify what articles we needed to buy either individually or collectively. For instance, the list specified that we needed three tents for Advanced Base Camp – the camp above Base Camp where we would store our food and equipment before carrying it further up the mountain. All those who had tents brought them along and erected them in the church hall. Then questions were asked. How easy would it be to pitch these tents on snow and glacial moraine? Were they big enough? Could we borrow more suitable tents from friends? How heavy would they be?

During the course of the day kilograms were a major concern. We had an assortment of bathroom and kitchen scales so that we could note the weight of each item on our master list together with pertinent comments. In the column marked climbing ropes, six needed, my brand new, sixty-metre, dry-treated Mammut 8.5 millimetre rope was unsurprisingly rated excellent. My twenty year old down sleeping bag was given the thumbs down. I'd need to buy a new one.

We did the weighing and note taking in pairs covering the floor with untidy heaps of ropes, slings, karabiners (metal links used to clip onto the rope and belay anchors), nuts and friends (metal chockstones and camming devices designed to lodge in cracks); boots, gaiters, crampons, ice axes, harnesses and helmets (ice-climbing gear) and clothes – thermal underwear, Goretex jackets, balaclavas, salopettes (chest high trousers), gloves and socks and so on. Roly had borrowed a camcorder and recorded the organised chaos on tape.

For light relief in the evening the team looked at Colin, Andrew and Titch's slides of the first Red Rope expedition in 1997 to climb the previously unclimbed peak CB11 in the Lahaul region of Himchal Pradesh in northern India. What made me cringe were the pictures of red raw high altitude sunburn suffered by the two 1997 expedition members who were not in the 2001 team. Colin emphasised the need to use loads of sun block throughout our trip and Titch was the only one to suffer sunburn when he forgot to apply sun cream on summit day.

Another thing I noted during the commentary and conversation surrounding the slide show was a certain degree of animosity felt towards one of these sunburnt individuals. I recalled a footnote in the CB11 expedition report, which mentioned the team's dismay at this climber's lack of teamwork. On the ascent of CB11 David had said he was cold and that to keep warm he would untie from the rope and solo alongside Andrew and Gurpal. Andrew felt distinctly worried about this decision because Gurpal, their keen but inexperienced Indian Liaison Officer, had displayed little knowledge of a safe belaying technique – the means by which you hold a fall on the rope. Disregarding this David soon left Andrew and Gurpal behind and ascended and descended the mountain alone. David's 'solo' ascent of the mountain was acknowledged to be a fine feat of mountaineering but his attitude and actions, which included clearing a stove from the bivvy site that was needed later, caused great ill-feeling. I hoped that our Tirsuli North Wall expedition would not be afflicted by such bitterness.

The following day the team 'enjoyed' its first training session. It was meant to include rock climbing in Derbyshire but pouring rain pursued us as we drove desperately from one crag to another. I dubbed it 'patience training' in readiness for what I envisaged would be the frustrations and trials of everyday expedition life. At least having admitted defeat in the face of the unrelenting British rain, we could console ourselves by visiting the gear shop in Hathersage. What consolations would there be half way up a glacier? (Morrison's mushroom soup with croutons was one!).

The designated role of each member of the team was confirmed this September weekend. Titch was in charge of food as on the 1997 CB11 expedition. Andrew was the treasurer and also collaborated with Chris Drinkwater who was responsible for equipment. Chris Smart assisted Andrew with the finances and organised the travel arrangements. Roly was the medical officer. Colin was the expedition leader and compiled the applications for the climbing permit and grants. It was suggested that I organise the training sessions with Titch's help. Cunning Colin thought I. He's suggested that I'm responsible for one of the things about which I lack confidence in order to boost my confidence.

Titch kicked the training ball off the mark with a questionnaire that highlighted the need for everyone to have an organised personal training schedule to maximise fitness. (I'd fortuitously joined a local gym at the beginning of 2000 and had begun a training programme).

This was followed by my compilation of a list of the team members' training needs so that they could be systematically addressed at training weekends. In November in groups of two or three, the team role-played different mountaineering problem scenarios. For example:

The leader falls in a crevasse and is knocked unconscious.

The terrain is hard ice under shallow snow. The lip of the crevasse is unstable.

You have a full rack of equipment. Rescue him/her.

The weekend was very successful because it gave everybody the opportunity to learn, practise, discuss and query procedures and techniques together. It was also a time when I thought money had dropped from the sky – I found twenty pounds in my bag that I couldn't account for but nobody else claimed. Eventually I realised it was cash I'd secreted away in one of my climbing books and forgotten about. This wasn't the last time I was to feel daft.

Other important issues we discussed that first September meeting, were whether we should take an altitude bag and oxygen. I was keen for us to take an altitude bag because my partner Brian had been told this equipment was important if anyone was stricken by altitude sickness. Another reason was the route that we expected to take when we left Base Camp involved ascending the 4500 metre (14,764 foot) high Surans Ka Dhura pass before descending to Malari. If anyone needed to be evacuated urgently due to acute mountain sickness an altitude bag could save his or her life. The team unanimously agreed that we'd go to the expense of either buying or hiring this equipment.

The next discussion concerned the use of oxygen on the climb or for medical purposes. My gut reaction was that if I was going to succeed in climbing a mountain I'd personally want to do it under my own steam or not at all. Oxygen was expensive and something else to carry and none of the team were enthusiastic for its use to assist climbing at altitude so it was decided none at all would be taken. I did wonder later if it might have been a good idea to include one or two bottles for medical aid but we didn't. At one point we contemplated not taking morphine on the trip but after passing on my pharmacist brother's view that someone suffering a severe injury would appreciate some strong analgesic Roly reconsidered. He'd been worried about the fiddliness associated with injecting things into each other and the fact that morphine suppresses breathing to some extent – not a very helpful side effect at altitude!

We did decide against taking avalanche transceivers because it took time to learn how to use them and they were very expensive, too. We were, after all, a very small party going to a remote glacier basin rather than the more accessible Alps. No rescue helicopters or fellow climbers would be at hand to help dig us out. The general consensus was fatalistic. If we were avalanched climbing the Tirsuli North Wall, we wouldn't survive, transceivers or not. It was strange to hear ourselves talking about possible death so nonchalantly. Did I really think I might die? Yes, the intellectual part of me recognised that there was a risk of dying on the expedition. In my farewell letter to Brian, who had taken the family to France before I left for India, I wrote:

> *Take good care of yourself over the next few weeks. It's a shame you always (or I always) tend to appreciate someone more when they're not with you. Maybe it's human nature. Anyway I do hope to come back alive*

and well after having a great time and if anything does happen remember I've had a good fifty near years.

I expelled from my mind the more horrifying possibility that I could lose a limb or be permanently paralysed and become a burden to my family. The optimistic part of me 'crossed its fingers' and trusted to good fortune.

So the team members ticked and crossed and annotated their various lists awaiting confirmation from the Indian Mountaineering Federation in New Delhi that the necessary permit had been granted. All mountaineering expeditions to India require a permit. We feared that our permit to a mountain near the Tibetan border, within what is designated the Inner Line Area, might be a little more tricky to secure. The key date November 30th came and went and no news arrived from India. I still hadn't heard whether I'd be allowed six weeks' leave from my teaching post. Maybe I wouldn't in the end need it.

It was that funny period between Christmas and New Year and I felt that I needed to blow the cobwebs away after an excess of sloth and indulgence. Did Chris and Colin fancy a walk in the Peak District? Despite blizzards warnings we decided we'd risk a trip up the motorway.

When I drove around to pick up Colin and Chris I was asked inside and handed a letter with the heading British Mountaineering Council/Mount Everest Foundation. The British Mountaineering Council administers UK Sport funding for expeditions attempting first ascents in remote mountainous environments. Applications are via the Mount Everest Foundation, which also provides grant opportunities. I read the letter, noting in particular the phrases, which referred to the board's view that the team had inadequate experience for such an objective as Tirsuli West. I swallowed and thought, "Bloody hell, they must know it's me that's going."

In a later paragraph there was a reference to it being highly unlikely that we would be granted a permit to climb Tirsuli West and it would be advisable to reconsider our objective and re-submit our grant application. I passed the letter back to Colin, shrugging my shoulders submissively, with the words, "Well, that's it, then."

"It's not!" flashed back Colin. "We're not leaving it at that!"

I wondered what we were going to do.

Apparently the expedition could still go ahead if the permit materialised but it would not have gained British Mountaineering Council approval or a British Mountaineering Council grant of £1600 and a Mount Everest Foundation grant of £640.

"Hmmm," I thought with some anxiety, "missing out on the money would be a blow but Brian would not be happy to hear about the lack of official confidence in the team's expertise. Mum's got to be the word on that score."

There was snow on the top of Stanage Edge in Derbyshire. The day was fine and crisp and there were no horrendous delays on the motorway. Colin, Chris and I had one of those magnificently invigorating winter walks along the gritstone cliff revelling in its sedate beauty. Worries about permits and grants were temporarily postponed until the New Year

* * *

I had just come back from my first day's ice climbing in North Wales with my brand new Mountain Technology ice hammer when this news arrived from Vishwas, the owner of the travel agency India Insight Tours, who was organising logistics in India.

DEAR COLIN

CONGRATULATIONS – I HAVE GOT THE PERMIT DONEEEEEE!!!!!!

I HAVE THE ORIGINAL IN HAND & THE SAME HAS BEEN FAXED TO INDIAN CONSULATE IN BIRMINGHAM AS WELL….TIME TO CELEBRATE FOR ALL OF YOU….U OWE ME A GOOD DRINK. PLEASE TELL ALL TEAM ….. WE GOT IT WELL IN TIME & ALSO THE EVEREST FOUNDATION IS IN FOR A SUR-

PRISEEEEEEEEE. CARRYING THE ORIGINAL WITH ME.

Colin's reply was, "Vishwas – You are a STAR!! See you Saturday. What's your favourite drink?"

At the team's next meeting copies of the permit were handed around and these words read out with great delight:

"British Expedition to Peak Tirsuli West (7035 M) 7 (Seven) members from 16.4.2001 to 27.5.2001...The above expedition has been cleared by the Ministry of Home Affairs, Government of India".

"Yippee! We're going to Tirsuli!" Titch wrote in the minutes.

We had lists. We had permits. But would we get any grants?

CHAPTER 7
"Good Luck!"

"Tempus fugit" and time raced by after the New Year. Following a long discussion the team decided that Colin would redraft the grant application letter highlighting the exploratory nature of our expedition and naming the unclimbed 6160 metre (20,210 foot) peak Chalab as our main objective. Fingers crossed this would be successful. (It was! We eventually received over two thousand pounds in grants.) The news that the permit had come through was swiftly followed by confirmation that I could have six weeks' leave from my school. Things were definitely looking up.

At the team's February meeting everyone was reminded about the importance of having dental check ups and ensuring feet were in tip top condition with no hard skin waiting to crack, bleed and fester on freezing cold Himalayan mountain slopes. We'd all made our own decisions about what injections we required and whether we'd take malaria tablets or not. I'd become a veritable pincushion and wondered how all the serum coursing through my veins didn't hopelessly curdle. Miraculously I only suffered one bad reaction.

We discussed training next. Roly had asked Rob Spencer, from Plas Y Brenin, the National Mountain Centre in Wales, to provide a first aid course tailored to our needs just before our departure so that everything we learnt would be fresh in our minds. The date set was the 31st March. The same date everyone had to give their passports and visa forms to me so I could go to the Indian Consulate in Birmingham and collect the visas.

We all dispersed to check our final lists. I bought shiny new jumars for ascending fixed ropes, which I never used. Chris Drinkwater got me a good deal on Paramo salopette trousers, chest high for greater warmth and with a padded, drop-down bottom flap to protect my bum on icy belay ledges and make going to the loo in cold wild places easier. I stocked up on lip salve and bought batteries for my Walkman. Every item was ticked.

* * *

On the 31st March Chris D. realised that he hadn't got the special Inner Line X visa form that he was meant to be handing to me. Mild panic ensued until we managed to download it off Roly's computer. My blood then ran cold when Colin said I should have a second piece of paper to go with the visa applications.

"No, Colin." I said emphatically. "I'm pretty sure this is the only piece of paper you gave me." (Gulp).

We were first-aided out. Let anyone dare get hurt. We'd sort them. There was a chuckle as the oft quoted Mark Twight, the author of the team's 'bible', the book called "Extreme Alpinism– Climbing light, fast and high" was quoted again.

Monday 2nd April I e-mailed the team the news, "We're all now the holders of the X Visa!"

More exciting e-mails were to be zinging and zanging back and forth during the following week. To my astonishment I saw an e-mail on my computer sent by the team's favourite mountaineer and author Mark Twight. Open-mouthed I read the following:

Subject: Good Luck!

Hi guys!

My buddy Rob Spencer tells me that you are going to the Kumaon soon to make an alpine attempt on the North Wall of Tirsuli. He also says that you have been taking a lot of advice from my book 'Extreme Alpinism'. I hope you find it useful. When you return perhaps you would be interested in helping me with the sequel I'm working on – I'll certainly have a lot to learn from you people if you succeed on such a challenging face as Tirsuli North Wall.

Good Luck. I'd love to hear how you get on.

With best wishes,

Mark Twight

This e-mail sent me rushing off to tell my partner Brian the news. Annoyingly he was singularly unimpressed.

I read Colin's response with keen interest.

Dear Mark

Many thanks for your kind thoughts.

We had a great course with Rob last weekend – he certainly knows his stuff. I think it's turned out to be a good decision to have that kind of course just before we go, but after all the gear's been bought, tickets, visas etc. as it helps with mental preparation. It also ties in with our philosophy that the most important thing about this expedition is that we all come back alive.

Your book proved to be something of a revelation to several of us. In the end what I took away wasn't the detail of your approach to situations but more the question of mental attitude. In particular it comes down to questions all the time about why one does things the way one does. In particular, why be scared of climbing at night?

The other thing that both you and Rob have brought to the party is the question of hydration. I can remember having a particularly torrid time on the Gervasutti Pillar (forced bivvy with no gear etc.) but looking back closely I think we drank next to no water for nearly three days. On the third day we recovered our proper bivvy gear from the base of the route and struggled uphill in the blazing sun to the Midi. The moment I was given a drink, I puked up into the nearest waste bin. Hindsight says that that was no surprise!

Anyway I'm sure I can speak for the whole team in saying that we'd be delighted to contribute in whatever way we can to your next book. Even better if it can have as seismic an effect as your last book. Please get in touch after May 29th.
Colin

The next e-mail was even more remarkable.
Mark Twight wrote:

Colin

Thanks for your reply. I have actually been chatting with my publisher about your expedition and we thought it would be a good opportunity to produce a 'coffee-table' style hardback based solely on your expedition, assuming of course that it's successful. I know that you're leaving for India fairly soon, but we may be able to provide an advance payment for you all in the next few days.

I'm also discussing with Roly the possibility of lending your team a lightweight digital camcorder. There may be scope for a documentary to accompany the book.

I hope you are interested in this proposal.

Yours,

Mark

I went in search of Brian again.

"Brian! You'll never believe this. Mark Twight's suggested we video the expedition and has offered advance payment. He's saying they might make a book out of it."

My son Max looked round vaguely interested in his mum's prospective fame. Brian frowned and said, "Well, I can't see how they can do that. There's hardly any time to draw up a contract. A publisher won't just dish out money like that." Brian knew about these things but I pooh-poohed what he said.

"Well, that's what Mark Twight's written and I presume he knows what he's talking about."

I didn't like to admit that I was worried that the thought of book and film royalties might encourage the team to push itself harder than was wise.

Andrew was the first to express some scepticism about the e-mails.

> *Dear All,*
>
> *Are we SURE that this is not a piss take!! Also somewhat worried to read Mark's comments about such a CHALLENGING climb and him having a lot to learn from us!!*

I recalled the vastly experienced, published mountaineer Martin Moran's comment to me in the Alps when I told him that I was a member of an expedition aiming to climb Tirsuli West. "That's an extremely hard technical route," he said.

Was someone taking the piss? Who would it be?

I guessed it was Titch. He was the joker.

"What makes you think it was Titch?" Colin queried Packing Day morn.

"Well, he's always joking," I said. No comment.

"Well, it's not me." I continued. "It's not you or Chris. It can't be Chris Drinkwater because he sent an e-mail saying, "Gulp!" and it's not Andrew because of his e-mail so it must be Titch. Or Roly?" Silence.

And the truth dawned.

Oh, what dupes and fools we piddling mountaineer Malvolios are!

And what a gloriously evil scam Roly had executed. Much to be disapproved for the time wasting and anxiety it provoked but then to be relished.

God himself had wished the expedition "Good Luck!"

CHAPTER 8
Let's Get Packing

It's strange to think that 'enveloping bags' were to be the cause of my only sense of frustration with Colin's leadership. I remember Colin standing firm in Titch's sitting room declaring that it was absolutely essential that we all brought three kitbags or enveloping bags to packing day.

"Are you sure?" I queried dubiously. Colin's argument was that Himalayan porters preferred to carry gear in kitbags rather than rucksacks. I'd been out and purchased one ex-Czechoslovakian army kit bag and knew that, weighing nearly three kilograms, it not only encroached seriously into my twenty-kilogram weight allowance but was expensive too. I found myself joining in the mutterings of dissension over afternoon tea.

Insurrection was averted however by the discovery of the trusty post office sack. They're cheap – well, actually ours came free – light and strong. One survived a tumble down a hillside. Another fell off the top of a land rover, avoided the roll into the gorge below and was retrieved unscathed. (Of course both contained my gear!). The post office sack is not reliably waterproof however and hours were spent touring Indian back street bazaars in search of plastic bags to solve this failing. We discovered that plastic bags (and string) were rare commodities in the Indian towns we passed through on our way to the mountains. This meant our last night in Joshimath, the outpost of civilisation in that it boasted a hotel, telephone lines and a post office, was spent cutting and making shocking pink plastic sheeting into inner plastic bag liners for our individual post office sacks. Temperatures rose slightly when it looked like we might not all get our fair share of sick pink plastic but no one came to blows.

Sunday the 8th April was Packing Day. Andrew and I were the first contingent (after Titch) to arrive at the quasi derelict, damp and smelly but very spacious Yorkshire mill house that had been hired for the final weighing, sorting and packing of all gear – personal and collective.

I'd already painstakingly gone through listing and weighing and packing my gear into rucksacks and kitbags. (I had the time because it was the school holidays). I knew I was within the weight allowance and could in theory get on the plane that afternoon. Hyper-organisation is not necessarily a good thing I was to discover when the trusty post office sacks were magicked into the packing equation and the weighty canvas kitbags dumped. I received an extra allowance of several kilograms and cursed the thought that I'd missed out on packing a second lightweight sleeping bag and extra packets of cashew nuts – my mountain treat food.

Somewhat lengthy discussions and at times confused and confusing comments were exchanged about whether you counted the weight of your plastic boots into the sum of your packing allowance or not. I had already decided that I was going to be wearing heavy items like my Paramo salopettes and plastic climbing boots when my baggage was weighed at the airport and then change into lighter clothes afterwards. This worked out fine for me and my forward planning avoided the sense of pressure and panic that threatened to overwhelm those who had had to leave difficult decisions about what particular gear to take until the day. At one point during the afternoon Chris Drinkwater was spotted surrounded by a mountain of equipment, head in hands, in an agony of uncertainty about which pieces of equipment to jettison and which to keep. The whole packing process was stressful for all of us because it was necessary to make decisions, which we feared could in the end prove crucial to the success of the expedition.

Andrew and I had the job of collecting together three climbing gear racks from the whole mass of climbing equipment the six of us had brought along. There was a lot of muttering and chuntering and umming and arring as decisions were made in a vacuum of knowledge about the climbing condition we would confront. We finally decided that we'd feel happier if we took a specialist climbing rack to complement the general ones. The climbing equipment was shared out between different sacks just in case any bags went astray. Every sack was painstakingly weighed and the weights totalled.

By late afternoon twenty-one weighed and labelled post office sacks were piled up in the middle of the mill house floor waiting to be transported to Titch's house. Relief. We were acceptably near the Swissair weight allowance. Tom, our UK support and driver, was due to arrive at five. We heaved the sacks outside the mill house and waited. Hopefully it wouldn't start to rain. The sacks weren't waterproof yet. I hadn't actually seen Tom's van but those who had, were not surprised at the delay. At twenty to six a big, old, battered, bulbous bonneted rickety green van came clanking to a halt at the side of us. Apparently there'd been a bit of trouble getting it started! We threw the sacks into the back, drove round to Titch's to unload and agreed the final plans for Departure Day.

"Tom, you do have AA and relay cover for the van, don't you?" I checked.

The plane was due to leave at 8.10 a.m. on Monday 16th April 2001.

CHAPTER 9
D – Day

"Where is Andrew?" Colin muttered as the airport clock ticked past half past six.

Tom's old van had done Titch, Roly, Chris D. and myself proud. We'd left Leicester at ten p.m. and arrived at Heathrow at one thirty a.m. – a smooth journey with comfy seats and funky music. We weren't going to miss the plane. Colin and Chris walked up to the Swissair check-in desk at five thirty, looking cool, calm and collected. They weren't going to miss the plane. But Andrew hadn't arrived. Nobody dared utter the thought, "If anyone's going to miss the plane, it'll be him." Had he spoken of arriving at about seven? Surely not. That was cutting things a bit fine.

"Has anyone got his mobile number?" Colin asked.

I had had it but where had I put the wretched piece of paper with it on. I searched through my hand luggage.

Colin and Titch went outside to see whether looking for him would make him materialise any faster. It obviously did, because when I went out with the mobile number that I had at last found, I spotted Andrew being bundled out of a car. He had arrived and was wondering what all the fuss was about.

"But there's plenty of time," he protested. "Chris and Colin said they weren't expecting to arrive until about seven."

By now the Swissair stewardesses were checking in our trolleys full of sacks. We anxiously loaded them one by one onto the scales. No problem. All the gear was safely stowed. No excess baggage to pay. Relief and elation. Let's go upstairs and get a cup of something before going through to the departure lounge.

It was while I was off changing out of my heavy salopettes that high drama took place in the airport coffee bar lounge. We were all keyed up now the expedition had begun in earnest. Andrew kept saying how excited he was and in his excitement didn't spot the tray of scalding hot coffee someone had put on the floor. He stepped on the edge of the tray and the coffee cup somersaulted spraying its boiling hot contents down inside his shoe. "Yow!" he shouted as he frantically pulled his shoe and sock off as quickly as he could. When I emerged from the Ladies, Colin was walking towards the Gents to check how the cooling down process was proceeding. Medical man Roly was with Andrew as he balanced on one foot with the other in the sink under the cold tap. We hadn't expected our first aid training to be required so quickly.

The unspoken thought was that this silly little accident could prove a serious threat to Andrew's bid to climb the mountain. The blister on Andrew's foot, just below the ankle joint where climbing bootlaces are pulled tight and the foot flexes, was big and nasty. Minutes ticked by and it really was time we went through to passport control. Roly decided that Andrew would need a wheelchair to get to the aeroplane. It was just too painful for him to walk. So a somewhat subdued Tirsuli North Wall 2001 expedition team boarded flight 801B to Zurich en route to Delhi.

If God had meant us to fly he would have given us wings. Flying isn't normal. I don't like it and expect every lift off and landing to be the death of me but it certainly gets you places fast. We were no sooner leaving London than we were looking for the right gate for the 12.10 p.m. flight to Delhi. Colin managed amidst the rushing about to e-mail Vishwas, our Indian agent who was due to meet us in Delhi, news of Andrew's injury. We meanwhile caught glimpses of Andrew, attended by Roly, being chauffeured about Zurich airport in a Popemobile style buggy. Why were they going in the opposite direction to us?

"Yes, well, this Swiss medic guy at the First Aid Centre gave us this special gel for burns," Roly explained as we all sat back in the huge, almost empty airbus ready to enjoy free drinks, free films and airfare food for the next eight hours. Andrew had a row of seats to himself and was beginning to feel more perky after the traumas of the day. He spent a long time trying to work out how to send a forty-pound bunch of Interflora flowers via the aeroplane Internet to his partner Sarah whom he'd left so abruptly at Heathrow.

"I never got to say goodbye to her properly," he sighed.

* * *

It was 7 p.m. and Radio 4 'Archers' time in England when our plane began its descent into Delhi airport. We were entering a different world. Here the time was 11.40 p.m. and it was dark and humid. We emerged from Delhi customs unchallenged and were greeted enthusiastically by a well set, smiling Asian man with a black moustache who embraced both Colin and Chris S. This was Vishwas.

"You've had a good journey?" he asked us. "And how is Andrew?" Andrew was being propelled slowly along in a wheelchair by a sad-faced Indian. The passageway from Customs to outside the airport was buzzing with people despite the lateness of the hour and motley men, both young and old, kept reaching for our trolleys and offering their services as porters. Vishwas tut-tutted them away and we eventually emerged into the bustling chaos outside with fume-belching buses reversing and advancing, bicycle rickshaws swerving in and out and bodies rushing and pushing, calling and shouting here, there and everywhere. A small, slight, mousy-faced man with a pencil moustache popped up and offered us orange garlands.

"Norbu! How good to see you again!" Colin cried out with delight. Norbu smiled bashfully. He had been Base Camp manager on the 1997 expedition to CB11 and was remembered with great affection. Each of us put the welcoming garlands around our neck and a group photo was taken beside our own special fume-belching bus. The post office sacks were flung in the back and we were off zipping along the quiet night Delhi streets to the posh and plush Park Hotel. We had arrived.

I had visited Delhi before. At eleven o'clock on the eleventh of May in 1978 I'd arranged to rendezvous with Cathy, a Voluntary Service Overseas volunteer I had become good friends with in Thailand, at the Delhi British Council offices. She was travelling in from Kashmir while I was arriving from Nepal. Our plan was to travel back to Britain together through Afghanistan, Iran, Turkey and so on. That was twenty-three years ago. How had the city changed?

Do you know I can't really say? All I can report is that I felt at home. I felt comfortable and at ease in the environment despite the heat and the dust and the grime and the hustle and the bustle and the incredibly smelly latrines just round the corner from the fragrant ivory-towered Park Hotel.

We had our first of many meetings in Colin and Chris' superior room on the fifth floor of the Park at 9 a.m. the following morning.

"Bloody hell! They've given you a fancy dressing gown. We haven't got one in our room!" I complained light-heartedly. The aim of the gathering was to check how everybody was feeling and to decide who would accompany Vishwas' sister, Pratigya, on a shopping trip to buy the list of supplies that we hadn't purchased in England. Roly informed us that the plan concerning Andrew's ankle was to keep it clean, covered and dry for about a week and hope for the best.

"Sorry, what was that you said?" Chris Drinkwater asked craning his head towards Roly sat on the opposite side of the room.

"What's wrong, Chris?" Colin interjected, his eyelids fluttering as they do sometimes when he speaks. "Can't you hear?"

"Well, umm... I haven't got my hearing aid so I don't

always catch what people say." Chris replied.

Colin looked at Chris. He has quite penetrating eyes. "You haven't got your hearing aid?"

"Well…" Chris cleared his throat. "No, I left it at home. It seemed… like one extra thing to worry about…" he coughed again, "… so I didn't pack it." Nothing more was said but I know everyone felt the silence.

At last it was decided. Titch, Chris Smart, Chris D., and I were off to the market with Pratigya (Vishwas' sister) in a very fine, black, four-wheel drive, chauffeur driven car. I was delighted because the market we wanted was miles away and we got a sightseeing tour of Delhi. The traffic was hectic and noisy as Delhi drivers hoot vigorously every time they overtake you but it felt like every one knew what to expect – especially the guy pulled over for jumping the traffic lights!

The items we bought included – dried fruit, nuts, 'La Vache qui Rit' processed cheese, (I love cheese), cous-cous, twelve metres of nylon string, batteries and twenty four cigarette lighters. Chris Drinkwater picked up some plastic bin liners and said, "Don't we need more of these?"

"Nah," the rest of us replied. "We've got enough." That was a stupid mistake but who would have thought plastic bags were as rare as gold dust and string in the conurbations of Northern India?

Unlike the rest of us, Chris D. had never been to India before. He was fascinated by the everyday scenes of Delhi street life and had his camera out clicking non-stop. At one point we all stood aghast as he dodged out into the middle of a busy road, crouched down and photographed a posse of stationery motorbikes parked on the other side of the street. Would this be the Rochdale Observer headline "Mountaineer Mangled in Motorbike Madness"? Pratigya found it all very amusing.

At last we agreed we had done what we could. We hadn't found a suitable set of tools or jerry can or bamboo poles to act as glacier markers but Vishwas would be able to sort that out for us later. At four in the afternoon Vishwas and Colin were due to meet the director of the Indian Mountaineering

Federation at his office. Who wanted to go along for the ride?

We were off on another interesting tour in a different direction past the commercial buildings of Connaught Circus, past old ladies perched on motorcycles, past the Presidential buildings, past ramshackle cardboard shanty towns, on and on until eventually we went through a gate and up a hill to a fort-like building with well kept gardens and an outdoor climbing wall. This was the Indian Mountaineering Federation. Colin and Vishwas went through to complete the official business with the director. I noticed a short, unsmiling, young-looking, slick-haired Asian man seated in an antechamber as they walked through but thought nothing of it.

Roly, Titch, Andrew and I went to look around the Federation's mountaineering museum and library. Then we came across postcards for sale featuring a Roger Payne photograph of Tirsuli West from the Bagini Barak side. We all bought several of these to send back home. The official business was taking a long time. We hoped nothing was wrong and wandered outside to the artificial climbing wall where a class of smartly clothed Indian schoolboys were seated on the grass watching a demonstration on how to abseil. We wandered back in and met Colin carrying a stack of about fifteen back copies of the Himalayan Journal that he'd bought. Everything was okay. We were then introduced to our Liaison Officer, the serious young man whom I'd noticed. His name was Momoraj and as he explained at a later date in the Park Hotel lounge; he was from Manipur, in the North East of India near the Burmese border, where people were Mongoloid in appearance. Momoraj spoke several languages including Hindi and Manipuri and had been above 6,000 metres (19,685 feet) on an Indian mountaineering expedition. I noted how superb his command of English was and how extensive his vocabulary. "He's an interesting man," I thought.

In the car on the way back to the hotel Vishwas gave his opinion of Momoraj.

"He's a serious guy. I've invited him to join us for a meal at my house tomorrow. A few whiskies down him should loosen him up."

"His English is very good and he's certainly intelligent," Colin commented.

Vishwas paused and then continued "Yes, that's good. He shouldn't cause us any trouble."

"You mean, he'll play with a straight bat," Colin laughed. There was no wish for a repeat of the problems that occurred with Gurpal, the Liaison Officer on the CB11 trip, who pressed to climb with the team while lacking the appropriate skills.

Momoraj didn't get to Vishwas' dinner however; and there was what Colin considered an unreasonable phone call from him expecting help with the transportation of his gear, so Momoraj was still regarded as a bit of an unknown quantity when we set out on the road two days later.

At our evening meeting that night we discussed whether we should hire walkie-talkies so we had some means of communicating with the outside world when we were at Base Camp. The hire cost was expensive. We had no guarantee the machines could cover the distance and height gain over the Surans Ka Dhura pass and who would there be to man the radio in Malari. Nobody. The decision was against walkie-talkies. I felt a twinge of anxiety at the thought of how isolated we would be in the event of trouble but the decision was made.

It was dinner at Vishwas' the following evening.

Vishwas' business is without doubt a family business. Pratigya was our taxi driver for the long journey to the suburbs and Vishwas' mother the provider of a vast array of delicious Indian dishes that seemed endless. Vishwas' wife, Monisha, supported him as hostess. We met the extended family and were shown with great pride volume after volume after volume after volume of Vishwas' younger sister's wedding photos. What a picture! What a photograph! Seven expedition team members politely clustered around huge and ornate photograph albums that appeared as endlessly as the food. A deeply serious intent ran alongside Vishwas' wish to entertain and divert with open and generous Indian hospitality. Towards the end of the evening he took the opportunity to go over our itinerary in some detail, to explain which Indian staff would be accompanying us and to wish our expedition every success and a safe conclusion. In a fortnight's time he was going to welcome a German team, which was attempting Tirsuli West from the Bagini Barak side, in a similar way. Norbu was going to accompany us as far as our Base Camp on the Siruanch glacier and then leave us in the capable hands of Base Camp manager Ranjit Singh so that he could go and supervise the Germans' camp. This was the start of the busy season for Vishwas and company.

With bellies bursting we were driven back, past lines of lit-up factory lorries setting off to make deliveries, for our last night of luxury before we hit the road.

CHAPTER 10
The Road to Malari

I had heard and read about the terrifying road journeys climbers and other travellers have endured on the Karakoram highway and other Asian routes to the mountains. Colin had graphically described the feelings of sheer horror and heart-stopping fear that he had experienced when hurtling straight for oncoming buses and teetering on the edge of plunging gorges in his CB11 expedition slide show and there was a whole paragraph about it in the report. "Even though the maximum speed of our bus was probably no faster than 80 kph, the driver managed to make the journey feel like a race and would overtake at every available opportunity, even if another vehicle was coming in the opposite direction. During all our time on the roads we saw the remains of many accidents and on far too numerous occasions, we thought our bus was to be involved in one." As I clambered onto our tourist bus outside the Park Hotel I wondered what our journey would be like. It would be a bit of an anti-climax to get killed before even reaching the mountains.

As it happened we had a bus driver who was the epitome of decorum on the road and he was ably assisted by the bus boy ever vigilant at his side. We didn't see a single accident and the ringing notes of the bus horn blasting as our driver swung out to overtake took on a soothing quality as we thundered up the highway. It struck me how like Thailand it was with the innumerable little stalls at the side of the road selling sweets and fizzy pop, assortments of exotic fruits, swathes of colourful materials and rusty bits of car and worn tyres. How on earth did they all make a living?

Chris Drinkwater had his camera out and soon gained a reputation for having a pig fetish. "How many photos of wild pigs have you taken now, Chris?" Titch teased him. Several times our chauffeur was forced to slow down by flooding and traffic congestion in the towns we passed through. The main street became clogged with gaily-decorated lorries, clapped out buses from which eyes often stared at us stonily, bone-shaking bicycles, tractors and carts, jeeps and cars, dogs and cows and people hurrying this way and that on business or exhorting us to buy their wares. The hours passed by as we gazed through the grimy windows at life passing by, or dozed, or chatted, or listened to our personal stereos, occasionally whipped by the bus' window curtains blowing in the breeze. All our gear was piled up at the back of the bus but there were still enough places left at the start of the journey for us all to have the luxury of two seats to ourselves. This would change when we picked up the rest of the Indian staff in Rishikesh, some eight hours or so up the road north of Delhi.

We had a brief sightseeing stop at the holy and touristy city of Hardwar on the banks of the river Ganges, which was characterised by the greatest amount of hassling for money by ragged and destitute children that we were to encounter the whole trip. One little girl approached to put a blob of mendhi (a reddish dye made from henna leaves), a sign of blessing, on my forehead, but I hard-heartedly waved her away. A little later Chris Drinkwater graciously gave her a ten-rupee note. Her face broke out into an enormous smile and she skipped away whooping with delight. I felt small in my mean-mindedness and was glad to be on the road again.

We were stopping the night at Rishikesh. That is, if we succeeded in gaining entry to the town. A policeman halted our bus at a road barrier on the outskirts, saying that the vehicle was too heavy for the road ahead and directed the driver to turn left up a side street. No problem we thought as we rattled and bumped ahead. Then a crowd of vociferous and gesticulating men swarmed in front of the bus and forced the driver to stop.

For the next twenty minutes there was to the non-Hindi speaker a life and death melodrama of arguing and shouting, fist clenching and pointing, back turning and shrugging as Norbu, Momoraj, the bus driver and the bus boy tried to effect a passage through to our hotel in the centre of town. At long last Norbu got twenty-two rupees (approximately 40 pence) out of his trouser pocket, bought a ticket from the loudest individual and our bus was waved through. What the palaver was about remained a mystery to all of us and once we actually arrived at the Rishikesh Hotel we wondered why we'd bothered. It was the pits.

One of the main reasons why Vishwas had chosen this night time stop was that it gave us tourists the opportunity to view a special Hindu religious ritual by the side of the river Ganges. As the sun began to sink crowds of the faithful flocked down to the riverside, purchased little leaf boats adorned with flowers and a candle balanced in the centre, lit the candles and then set the boats afloat on the holy Ganges water. Norbu, Momoraj, Colin and Chris Drinkwater all participated in the ceremony launching their tiny vessels into the darkness. I watched anxiously as some of these fragile crafts danced crazily on the ripples in grave danger of capsize. Some spun round and round in eddies making no progress whatsoever, then tipped over and scattered their petals on the river's waters. The candles of others spluttered and coughed and died in seconds. Others joined other triumphantly flickering boatlets bobbing resolutely and brilliantly seawards. Norbu offered me one of these pretty little boats to set afloat but I declined for a confusion of reasons. I think one was that I don't own to any religious faith and felt uncomfortable about joining in the rites of a faith I didn't embrace. Another could have been the fear that my little boat might be immediately shipwrecked and what would that have symbolised?

On the way back to the hotel from the riverside Momoraj and I chatted a little about two closely related topics, the food of the body and the food of the soul. I learnt that the traditional Manipuri speciality is chilli fish and that Momoraj was a liberal Hindu who valued and respected all the religions of the world. Again he struck me as a thoughtful and sensitive man. I had read much about the trials and tribulations some mountaineering expeditions have experienced with their Liaison Officers and had looked forward with interest to meeting ours. Theirs is not an easy role I imagine to perform well. They must try and form a diplomatic, understanding bridge between two essentially very different cultures and seek to satisfy the desires and demands of both mountaineers and Ministry. How would Momoraj serve us we asked ourselves?

* * *

By 6 a.m. the following morning we were on the road again.The Indian plains were left far behind us now and our route rose steadily following the bends and curves of the river winding its way along the gorges far below us. I had remembered to take my travel sickness pills so I was able to enjoy the magnificent views. We passed slim, saried women carrying hay loads on their heads, dark-skinned workers cutting corn with glinting scythes and a gigantic Hindu statue guarding the way. Someone spotted monkeys in the roadside trees – big chimpanzee grey ones and a little later, smaller ones with green backs.

We stopped at a hillside village while the bus driver and his boy had breakfast and I experienced my first 'crouching loo' for many years. Many public conveniences were sampled on our trip and all, bar the foul-smelling ones outside the Park Hotel in Delhi, were of a reasonable standard. Our bus was much more crowded now with the addition of seven Indian staff. Roly and I shared a seat and taped music – the soundtrack from the film "O Brother! Where art thou?" We'd both enjoyed the film and I couldn't help recalling the hilarious scene where George Clooney's sidekick believes his friend has been changed into a toad.

It was after our lunch of rice, dahl (lentils) and saag paneer (spinach and cheese) curry that Andrew looking a tad green confessed to feeling poorly. "Just a few more hours and we'll be at Joshimath," were someone's words of comfort.

Back on the bus again we continued our climb along winding mountain roads with precipitous drops on my side! Snow-capped mountains were visible in the distance. It couldn't be far now!

It was ten past six in the evening when the bus finally drew up at the Dronagiri Hotel in Joshimath. By this time Andrew was looking distinctly off colour. Roly and Chris Smart diagnosed the gut infection 'giardiasis' and Andrew retired to his room with medical man Roly who was also feeling unwell. While the Indian staff were in the throes of unloading the bus we were introduced to Kundan Singh Ravat, the porters' agent. He was a short, stocky, round-faced man with a small black moustache, wearing a voluminous luminous yellow Goretex jacket. He organised the employment and organisation of porters for us with the head porter, his slighter but more inebriate brother, Raju. The name Kundan Singh rang a bell and I asked if he knew Martin Moran, the mountaineer who'd run my alpine training course. Kundan's face lit up and he beamed out, "Martin very good man...coming soon." Yes, he was organising an expedition to climb another mountain in the region called Trisul.

It was a quiet evening meal at the Dronagiri Hotel. We met Ranjit who was going to be our Base Camp manager. He was a tall, strong, dependable-looking, Tibetan featured man, softly spoken and diffident. I will always remember with warmth the powerful grip he took of my wrist when he helped me ford the Malari river our last evening there. Feeling indisposed,

Andrew and Roly didn't appear for dinner. As for me I had a headache and took an aspirin before I went to bed.

Saturday 21st April 2001

Good breakfast – chips, cheese, omelette. I woke about 6 a.m., lay in bed until 7.30. Colin off to check permit. Problem with Sub-Divisional Magistrate's personal assistant. Colin and Momoraj had to go to Chomali. I suggested telephone first but Colin said better go in person. Unfortunately it turned out they missed the Sub-Divisional Magistrate who had actually come up to Joshimath!

While Colin and Momoraj were on their wearing and frustrating wild goose permit chase to Chomali (two hours jeep drive back down the mountain roads) the rest of the team, save Andrew who was still feeling weak, went shopping for the last few essentials with Ranjit.

Joshimath is a small mountain town with basically one main street lined with many, mostly wooden, shopping booths. The five of us tagged along after Ranjit who checked what we required and then negotiated the prices. We were satisfied with the big blue plastic barrel we bought for the beer kit, content with the sweets and chocolate bars Roly felt were a necessary addition to our high altitude lunch supplies but disappointed as regards plastic bags. In retrospect the dearth of these polluters of the environment is no bad thing but it was a pain at the time.

There was afternoon tea and cake when we got back to the hotel. Norbu and Ranjit hovered around us pouring tea, passing sugar and cutting cake. It was unnerving being waited on hand and foot in this alien manner but I accepted it as being the rules of the game in this type of expedition context. In hiring Vishwas as our agent we had taken on the whole 'Mem Sahib' caboodle reminiscent of British rule in India and had to accept being treated in an unnervingly respectful manner by the Indian staff. As we ate and drank

Colin wearily recounted the frustrations of his day, which included the obstructive attitude of the Sub-Divisional Magistrate's personal assistant and the hectic and fruitless jeep ride. He said how impressed he'd been by Momoraj's handling of a difficult diplomatic situation. Tomorrow he and Momoraj would have to delay coming on the proposed acclimatisation trip on the cable car to Auli so that another attempt could be made to get our permit sanctioned by the Sub-Divisional Magistrate.

Andrew was feeling a lot better that evening. In fact he'd managed to bowl a few balls during the late afternoon cricket match with Ranjit, Norbu and the other staff on the hotel veranda. (One of our most important purchases that afternoon had included a fine wooden cricket bat and two balls.) His ankle, as well as his guts, was definitely on the mend. Roly had e-mailed his Doctor dad in England to check-up on the treatment and it looked like a lancing of the blister was due soon. During the meal Andrew mentioned that one of the hanging stoves didn't work properly when he and Roly had tested it. "Uh-oh, does this spell trouble?" No. Colin asked a couple of diagnostic questions and recognised the fault was in the operating of the stove rather than the stove itself. Rest easy, comrades. Unfortunately I suddenly felt a wave of nausea sweep over me and couldn't rest easy at all. I dutifully sat through Roly's first aid meeting about the contents of our individual first aid packs feeling like death and then retreated to my bed to die.

The 14th July 1971 doesn't exist for me. It was the day I lay in a coma in a Florentine hospital caused by meningitis (caught from kissing my Italian soldier boyfriend some speculated). Fortunately Doctor Cappelli saved me by diagnosing the infection early enough for me to be given life-saving antibiotics. Ever since that time however I've been inclined to imagine the worst when struck by illness. Consequently when I retired to my room that evening I began to imagine I had some dreadful disease. I felt sick. I felt drained of all energy. I had a headache and then I had an excruciating backache. I turned and tossed but couldn't sleep. Did I have a uterine infection? Had I forgotten to remove a tampon in the excitement of the trip, which was slowly festering away up there? That would be a fine state of affairs to have to admit to. Investigation proved negative however. I didn't sleep a wink all night and crawled out of bed for breakfast feeling VERY BAD.

Colin and Chris were seated at the breakfast table when I sank down in my chair that sunny Sunday.

"How are you this morning?" they asked cheerfully.

"Not so good. I didn't sleep at all. I've got a terrible backache and I seem to have a period that's going on forever." With effort I slowly drank a cup of tea and listened as the others discussed what time to set off to catch the Auli cable car.

"Are you going, Ange?" Colin asked.

"I don't know," I replied, "I want to but I don't feel at all well."

"Well, you could consider going up and just lying down when you get there so as you get the benefits of acclimatising at 3000 plus metres." I smiled wanly and wondered about this proposal. It would be more interesting than just lying in the hotel bedroom. I'd be with the others, I'd be acclimatising and I hate missing out on anything, so I tottered along after the other five while Colin and Momoraj disappeared in the opposite direction permit-chasing.

We had a long wait for the cable car to swing into action. I stood and I sat. I sat and I stood feeling most uncomfortable. Indian family groups began to appear, walking towards the cable car station, which was at the top of a hill off Joshimath's main street. It was the start of the Indian holiday season. Soon Joshimath would be swarming with tourists from all over the continent. A very friendly Bengali family insisted on taking a photograph of Chris Smart and myself because we apparently added a bit of exoticism to the setting. I did my best to smile. At last the cable car set off up the hillside and in the distance Nanda Devi came into view. Here I was standing in this Indian cable car gazing towards this most famous mountain but it didn't make me feel any better.

Once at the top station, we disembarked and emerged into the sunshine. There we could marvel at the magnificent panorama that included other mountain giants such as Kamet and Dhauligiri. Roly, Andrew, Titch and the two Chrises pored over the maps exclaiming with pleasure every time they succeeded in pinpointing another summit. It was beautiful. Here was I surrounded by famous Himalayan Mountains but I felt so ill I could scarcely appreciate the beauty or the moment.

The main aim of the excursion was to acclimatise to the decrease in oxygen at this higher altitude. After some time gazing in wonderment at the scenery everyone got ready to walk into the surrounding hills. I began to follow but soon had to recognise that I was not physically up to it. "See you later folks," I called with false cheer as I turned around. I felt wretched and couldn't stop shedding a few tears as I picked my way slowly back to the cable car station.

I must have been lying outside that building, curled up on my sleeping mat for about five hours when I sensed someone looking at me. There were Colin and Momoraj. Having asked how I was, they were enigmatic about their meeting with the Sub-Divisional Magistrate when I enquired. I explained that I was waiting for the others to come back and wished them well for their walk. I knew I had no strength to join them.

The cable car ride back to Joshimath was marred by the loud, manic prattlings of an Indian man who rattled on in a mixture of Hindi and English about "softies" and "smarties" and "sweeties" and "dundars". Even if I hadn't known that "dundar" means "penis" in Hindi I would have gathered from the tone and manner of speaking that he was being an offensive boor. As we walked away from the lower cable car station our Bengali acquaintance came rushing after us to apologise for the man's rudeness. Alas, you meet that kind of ignorance all over the world. Happily you also meet a great generosity of spirit such as the Bengali's.

The worst of my sickness was over by the following day. I'd slept well. My backache had developed into frothy, spurty, watery diarrhoea, which suggested my system was rejecting whatever had been upsetting it and I was feeling almost human again. Just as well. There was a lot to be done.

The whole morning was spent checking and re-packing the post office sacks into twenty-five kilogram loads. My job was to list the contents in each sack so that we'd know what was lost if one fell down a ravine or into the river. We'd all put to the back of our minds the news that the Sub-Divisional Magistrate was still with-holding his permit to cross the Inner Line and had refused a photographic permit.

Afternoon tea was at 5 p.m. There were two pieces of important news to hear. Momoraj, our Liaison Officer, had okayed the decision to proceed to Malari the following day despite the Sub-Divisional Magistrate's vacillation. He took the view that we'd received permission from the central governing body in Delhi, the Indian Mountaineering Foundation, and this should be enough. Roly's report back from his visit to Joshimath Hospital was that it was a dreary, grubby, nasty, desolate place and he desperately hoped no one would get hurt. "Comforting news," I thought.

It was some time later when Chris D. and I were lying on our beds dozing that Andrew burst in saying that we needed photographs for the Sub-Divisional Magistrate's permit. Of course, duplicate passport photos of self had been on one of the master lists so I had mine. Off went Andrew, Chris D. Momoraj and Chris S. to find the town photographer. Everyone except Momoraj got back for the evening meal. We were just about to finish the egg custard pudding when he arrived looking flustered.

"Another problem," he sighed, "the Sub-Divisional Magistrate says all the staff need permits too. They've all got to go and get their photos taken. We might be late leaving tomorrow." We all inwardly groaned. This was getting beyond a joke. Colin passed around a courtesy letter that he'd written for the German expedition team that would soon be following us up to Joshimath. It included what might prove helpful information concerning our difficulties with the Sub-Divisional Magistrate and good wishes for their attempt on Tirsuli West from the other side. To say there was not a slight sense of rivalry would be inaccurate. To say there was a feeling that we were the poor relations had some truth in it. The German team had all 'mod cons'. They had a satellite phone! Would they succeed where we failed?

At ten o'clock that night in Joshimath, about 6 p.m. in Leicester, I made what I knew would be my last phone call home for three weeks. There were no phone lines in Malari and we didn't have a walkie-talkie let alone a satellite phone. Brian answered and told me that the whole family including the children, my mum, my brother, my nephew and my sister-in-law were all just about to start dinner. The telephone had rung and my sister-in-law had said, "Wouldn't it be nice if that was Angela!" And it was. It was enough to bring a lump to your throat.

The day came to a close with some excitement. Chris Drinkwater caught a buzzing hornet kamikazying around our bedroom deftly in a glass and then I fell asleep to the sound of barking mad dogs.

* * *

Now we really were on the road to Malari.

I was sat in the 'superior' jeep squashed between Momoraj, Chris Smart, Colin and the driver. It was the most delightful journey along a bumpy, partially metalled, single-track mountain road high above the steep-sided gorge of the Dhauli Ganga River. Mountains towered above us. Clusters of stone and wooden houses nestled on the hillsides. We passed fine-featured bronzed women carrying bales of hay and land tiered so that it formed an intricate pattern of green terracing. After about an hour and a half the jeeps pulled up at the side of a giant glistening red earthy mound, which was we were told, and could soon smell, a hot water spring.

We clambered carefully to the top of it and dipped our hands into the bubbling pool of sulphurous water. "Would you use my camera and take a photo of me?" Momoraj asked. I did praying it would come out.

We travelled on. The land became more barren as we passed Lata, the home village of Kundan and Raju Singh, and the four thousand metre (13,123 foot) high peaks Chotakana and Pharchola. We were at last rounding the final few bends in the road, approaching the outskirts of the village of Malari, when the army camp came into view and Momoraj decided that it might be politic to stop off and formally introduce himself to the army commander.

Four or five shabbily dressed, unshaven but good-humoured soldiers emerged from their wooden barracks as we climbed up the hillside from the road. Within minutes a tray of water and sweet milky tea had arrived which tasted as divine as holy nectar after the rigour and dust of the journey. There was a lot of eyeing up and nattering and coming and going but in the end the mission was aborted and we continued up the road to our camping ground just outside Malari. The army captain was based at the top of the hillside and our jeep driver categorically refused to take his jeep up the hill track. Momoraj conceded defeat gracefully.

At the litter strewn camping ground Andrew, Titch, Chris D. and Roly were comfortably established in their tents when we turned up. Who was going to share with whom?

"I'm happy to share with you, Momoraj, if you don't mind," I said boldly, disregarding any concerns about cultural taboos. I trusted that he would say something if it was a problem for him. He said nothing. So Colin and Chris Smart were able to share a tent together and I was given the opportunity to get to know a little more about Momoraj.

As for Malari – it was like a ghost town.

CHAPTER 11
Roly's Dream

Do you remember those spaghetti westerns where the cheroot-chewing, horse-riding hero cautiously paces past the rundown, wooden shop fronts of a dust-blown and near deserted Wild West town? Maybe there'll be an old-timer creaking back and forth on his rocking-chair who glances up with rheumy eyes or a scar-faced man who turns his back as soon as he spots the stranger. Well, I felt a bit like Clint Eastwood as I walked down main street Malari.

I sauntered down there alone because the others had gone earlier in the afternoon while I was relaxing in the tent with Puccini's 'Turandot', Sebastian Faulk's new novel and my diary. The first obstacle was the river that crossed the road before dropping steadily downwards to join the Dhauli Ganga in the gorge below. I took off my shoes and socks and waded across. "Brrr, it was cold!" Then I turned the bend in the road and saw the wide, dusty and disturbingly quiet street before me. "Do not forsake me, oh my darling," echoed faintly in my ears as I walked on wishing perhaps that I'd joined the earlier scouting parties.

As Chris Smart had told me, Malari consists of a lot of old, wooden and somewhat dilapidated houses. There are the remains of some finely carved balconies but not many. I was intrigued by the white and red chair outlines that were painted on the outside of many of the shacks and never got it confirmed whether these represented the number of rooms or toilets in the house or something entirely different. I noticed one or two fellows standing in the shadows of the houses as I approached the courtyard to a wooden temple. Large pictures of the monkey god Hanuman and the goddess Durga, seated on a tiger, were painted on the whitewashed walls. There were no worshippers however. I regained the main street and passed a huddle of men collected around a brazier outside a gloomy opening. "Namaste," I said gamely using the Hindi greeting but they stared back silently. At the far end of the village was a small rectangular area surrounded by stone benches. I wondered if this was the village meeting place. Two or three men were seated there and watched me as I went past. As I walked on feeling very conscious that my movements were being noted I thought desperately, "What do I do next?" It felt totally inappropriate to just turn around and walk back so I followed a dirt path leading up the hillside. After a little while I did turn around and looked down on the collection of small wooden and mud houses, which made up this picturesque but eerily silent, road head village. I didn't realise that when we returned in three weeks Malari would be utterly transformed into a humming community of busy, bustling, hard-working, laughing, joking men, women and children with their cows and their goats and their donkeys and their sheep.

The sky was clouding over now so I decided to retrace my steps. Back at the camping ground Andrew (his foot quite healed) was playing cricket with Ranjit, Norbu, Tashi and Kalu (the two cook boys) and a few porters who had started to arrive for our trek to Base Camp in two days. (Yangjor, the cook, rarely emerged from his cavernous cook tent during the whole expedition). I sat down with the rest of the team on the little veranda where our meal table was set up. 'Chai', a nice cup of tea, was due to be served at five. Looking lugubrious, Roly was moaning about being bored and having nothing to do. "I wish we could get up and go tomorrow," he sighed. "I don't understand why we have to hang around here for another whole day." I remembered hearing Andrew complaining about being bored and wanting to move on earlier in the day. (I put it down to short attention spans).

"I thought the idea was that a stop here would help us acclimatise, " I said as Tashi brought over the huge teapot.

"Yes, I know that's the idea but I'd rather be up there acclimatising not down here. I had this dream the other night." There was a pause while mugs were dished out, tea poured and biscuits passed around.

"Come on, then, Roly," Titch said at last. "What was this dream?"

"I dreamt," he paused. "I dreamt we never get to Base Camp."

We all smiled at him and laughed but he wasn't joking.

* * *

"Who's got a first aid kit handy?" Colin asked as the porter with the bleeding finger was ushered towards us. Dreams and nightmares were banished from Roly's mind as he jumped to the rescue in medical mode. "More blood than major damage," was the final diagnosis when, having cleaned up the wound, he applied the sticking plaster. It was late evening now and jeep doors kept banging as more and more porters kept arriving from down the valley. Our injured porter was so drunk that he had forgotten to remove his finger when he slammed his jeep door shut. I do believe he was Raju's brother.

I decided to walk down to the Malari River for a quick wash and bumped into Chris Drinkwater and Andrew on my way back. We went for a stroll up the road and watched shooting stars dive brightly across the dark skies. It was a beautiful clear night with the air so clean and fresh that it felt and smelt sublime. What a wonderful place to be – a totally different universe to home.

Momoraj was well tucked up in his sleeping bag when I got back to the tent. There had been some mix-up at the Indian Mountaineering Federation offices so Momoraj was less well equipped than desirable. He was wearing all his clothes and jackets in bed because his sleeping bag was thin and he had no head torch. I felt sorry for him. I was as snug as a bug in a rug in my expensive goose down bag. It wasn't fair.

We chatted for some time. He told me how he had only just returned to Delhi after visiting his family in Manipur, when he was assigned to our expedition, and the logistical problems that this had caused him. There had been a rickshaw strike in Delhi and this had made transport across town difficult. He went on to describe where he lived in Delhi and how difficult it was to get decent living accommodation. He'd done some teaching in Manipur but had then decided to go into government service. As I understood it he worked for the Intelligence Department. Titch's final verdict was that Momoraj was a spy but unsecret-agentlike he seemed very happy to talk about himself and asked little about me. The news that Deep Purple and Pink Floyd were two of his favourite bands could have been code I suppose but I never cracked it.

Momoraj's last piece of information before we slept was disappointing. Indians don't use the Hindi "Shuvrati" (Sleep tight) they stick to the boring old English "Good Night" without the coda – "Sleep tight. Don't let the bed-bugs bite!"

* * *

Roly and Andrew were happy. They were occupied. We were on the move if only for the acclimatisation walk to explore the start of the route up to the glacier.

Colin had done his research. He knew that historically there had been three ways of gaining entry to the Siruanch valley and glacier. The one used by most previous expeditions and the one that we would probably use involved crossing the high Surans Ka Dhura pass (c4500m/14,764ft) and descending the other side onto the Siruanch glacier.

We set off up the steep hillside that I had sampled the day before. It was a lovely walk with snowy mountains surrounding us, the river far below and miniature irises beginning to emerge from the soil with the coming of spring.

It was following the pause in the pine forest that my equilibrium was unsettled slightly. I had disappeared on a call of nature and after initially feeling smug about the settled nature of my bowels I'd become frustrated by the Indian cigarette lighter refusing to burn the toilet paper. When I eventually returned to the idyllic picnic spot under the pines Colin and Chris S. told me that the boys had gone on ahead. As I pressed on after them hoping to catch up the path became less clear. I turned to the right and soon found myself in a steep and overgrown gully. No sight or sound of anyone, anywhere. I began to climb and clamber upwards thrashing my way through clutching brambles and tearing branches.

"Where the hell are they and where's the bloody path?" I muttered under my breath.

At last I broke through a thorn bush and found myself on an obvious track leading upwards into more trees. I looked around and to my horror saw Colin and Chris far below walking up a totally different path.

"Help! Wrong path!" I cursed, then called, "Colin! Chris!" They turned around and waving my ski poles, I hollered, "I'm up here! But I'm coming down!!"

And I galumphed down that gully as quickly as I could and followed them. We continued to climb on upwards into another pine forest where the snow-covered path revealed recent footprints. This path led to a very steep and unstable scree slope. It was late in the day and the weather was changing so Colin, Chris and I turned around. A short time later as I've already described we met up with the boys and lost Chris Drinkwater when he continued down another path unaware that Titch, Andrew and Roly had descended to our path. A further drama on the long and tricky trek down was that Chris Smart badly wrenched her knee and Colin felt sick.

There was serious talking to be done that evening. While Colin rested in his tent Andrew, Titch and Momoraj discussed the route into the Siruanch glacier with Raju, the head (but frequently brainless-because-of-drink) porter. Raju mentioned the low route, which involved an eight kilometre walk along the road leading out of Malari to a spot called 'Point Eight'. The mountaineer, Harish Kapadia had referred to this in his 1984 article 'In Famous Footsteps'. The high route up to and over the Surans Ka Dhura pass and from there descending to the Siruanch glacier was the one we had considered being most feasible. After a long, involved discussion with Raju it was eventually agreed that the high route would be the best route to the glacier and next day we'd move camp to a terraced area called Camp Choping at (c3800m/12,303ft). We could approach the Surans Ka Dhura pass from there.

Colin had recovered by the end of supper but there was a lot of concern about the condition of Chris Smart's knee. Roly prescribed Ibruprofen and rest and we all crossed our fingers that the swelling and pain would settle down by the following day.

It had been a fraught evening but it came to a good-humoured and relaxed end with everybody contributing to a ribald tale of sex and rivalry starring Bananaman, a bounder called Geoffrey and the fair Esmeralda. The following day would bring us one day closer to Base Camp we thought.

***

"Angela's crap?"

"No, Angela's track!"

We were all sat in the mess tent at Camp Choping nestled underneath the magnificent cirque of the near six thousand metre (19,685 foot) high peak Kunti Bhannar discussing amongst other things the trek from Malari to Camp Choping.

The morning had begun unnervingly with about forty-five porters of all ages, sizes and demeanours, sporting the most extraordinary assortment of headgear ranging from bright red fluffy tea cosies to khaki balaclavas to granny's old flowery curtain material twirled into turbans, crouched down in a long line above us watching us eat our porridge.

At ten past eight we forded the Malari River with the porter vanguard and taking some steps up through the village eventually joined the path we had trodden on our acclimatisation walk. It was hard walking. Porters weighed down with our bulging sacks, metal boxes holding the kitchen equipment, plastic containers and blue barrels niftily passed me. I walked with Momoraj some of the time. The boys were ahead. Colin was supporting Chris whose sore knee made her progress slow. No matter.

One by one the porters came to a halt beside the old stone water tank where we had first noticed Chris Drinkwater's disappearance the day before. I presumed we'd stopped for a little rest when a murmur ran through the throng and I noticed a distressed Norbu rushing up the path wringing his hands wildly. I looked to Momoraj in his bright red jacket and sunglasses huddled up against the wicked wind that whipped around that corner of the hillside. "What is it?" I said. I could make no sense of the flood of Hindi.

"We've come the wrong way." Momoraj translated. "We should have turned right at the gully just after the pine forest."

Disheartened we all turned around and began filing back along the steep path. I met Colin and Chris on the way. "Looks like we've got to go up the path that I found yesterday," I explained. Colin wondered why Raju hadn't described the route more accurately to our porters. Chris groaned at the thought that she had done more distance than necessary and then laughed at the irony that the right track was yesterday's wrong track.

"No, Roly. I didn't say Angela's crap," she protested as we drank much appreciated tea after securing the tents with fixing ropes and rocks on the windswept terrace. "I said we walked up 'Angela's track!'"

The first afternoon and evening at Camp Choping was spent relaxing with Don Giovanni in the tent (only the opera, alas!), admiring and using the stone loo Titch and Roly had erected a disputed number of metres from the tent (Roly insisted it was only fifty metres away from the tents whereas others protested it was at least one hundred and fifty!) and playing Titch's Tick-Tock game. This involved passing the saltcellar and pepper pot to each other in opposite directions to the chant of tick-tock. It caused hysterical mayhem and sent us all off to bed exhausted. The following day we were due to accompany the porters up to the Surans Ka Dhura pass. It looked like action stations.

CHAPTER 12
Frustrations Mount

"It's inertia, that's what it is!" Andrew grumbled into his breakfast of cornflakes and omelette conjured up by the amazing cook Yangjor on this 3,800 metre (12,139 foot) high plateau with the nearest running water half an hour's walk away. We were all together in the mess tent and Andrew was complaining about Raju's non-appearance. It was nearing eight o'clock and as before he was keen to be on the move. Confidence in our head porter's organisational abilities had been seriously undermined by the previous day's confusion regarding the route.

"I mean we've got plenty of mountaineering experience between us," Andrew continued. "It's pretty obvious we go over that pass there." He put his mug of tea down, turned and waved towards the steep snow-covered slopes behind him. It had snowed heavily during the night. "I say we go over Andy's pass," he declared emphatically.

I looked in the direction he pointed and thought, "I haven't got a clue which way is the right way to go. Surely these local guys know something." To Andrew I said,

"Things are going to schedule so far, Andrew. We're having a good time. Why don't you relax a little?"

Colin sat listening to the exchange of views. He understood that some gear had been left in Malari by mistake and Raju was sorting the problem out. He suggested that we have a 10 a.m. deadline. If Raju hadn't appeared by then we would act.

At eight forty-five the slight, turquoise-topped, denim-jeaned, unshaven Raju arrived at Camp Choping. ("Jeans in the mountains!" I gazed amazed. "These guys were tough!") Being the keeper of the lists, I helped Colin and Andrew sort the sacks. The porters loaded themselves up and by ten o'clock we were all setting off up the steep, steep slope towards the Surans Ka Dhura pass. We all went at our own pace. I overtook Chris Smart who was still troubled by her sore knee. Roly was behind me for a while and then plodded past. At 4165 metres (13,665 feet) I caught up with Roly, Titch, Andrew, Chris Drinkwater, Momoraj, Norbu and Ranjit taking a rest. Our destination was out of sight in the distance along the ridge. We were surrounded by magnificent mountain peaks and photographed each other enthusiastically. Then we had to press on. The others steadily pulled away from me as the snow got deeper and the air got thinner. I urged Momoraj to go on ahead while I considered whether I could continue or should turn back. Having rested a short time I followed on only to bump into Colin on his way back from the Surans Ka Dhura.

"How far is it, Colin?" I asked breathlessly.

"About forty minutes, Ange."

It would be a long forty minutes for me I thought, feeling as weary as I did.

"Okay if I descend with you?" I checked.

And within seconds we were whizzing down the snow slopes at a terrific rate. Occasionally in my eagerness I found myself falling flat on my face and feeling foolish and once, one of my legs sunk so deep into the snow I could barely get it out. A little later I looked around to see Titch, Andrew, all the others and the porters charging down the slopes after us, leaping and bouncing, jumping and sliding with glee.

In contrast Colin would go at full speed for a burst of time and then pause. His theory was acclimatisation is assisted if you pause on the descent rather than rushing down non-stop. I adopted this strategy until the very end when I did a little sprint so that I wouldn't be the very last person back home to the tents. (We all have our pride!).

Two problems were discussed over afternoon tea.

Chris Smart was worried that *she* wouldn't be able to manage the snow conditions with her knee. Colin was concerned whether *anyone* would manage the snow conditions!

The climbers, who'd reached the Surans Ka Dhura pass, had observed with much alarm a number of huge cornices hanging threateningly over the avalanche prone east-facing snow slope our party would have to traverse to descend towards the Siruanch glacier.

* * *

If I were a thinly-clad Kumaoni or Nepali porter huddled in one small tent with forty others I'm sure that I would sing folk songs all night to keep myself warm and in good cheer. That's what our porters did during the long cold early hours of Saturday 28th April. Well, they had a rest day ahead of them! It was just eight high altitude porters and we six climbers who were going up to the Surans Ka Dhura for a second time to gauge the conditions and fix ropes. Chris Smart was going to rest her knee and Momoraj having suffered a sleepless night was remaining at camp.

We were up and off by 7 a.m. I felt tired and stiff, distinctly rough in fact. I decided to follow Colin who, unlike the others, was striking out more directly for the ridge. He's a very experienced and clear-thinking mountaineer who'd learnt a great deal about route finding on the Cuillin Ridge in Skye. As I mentioned that morning, on the long plod upwards, I had a lot of faith in him. There were a number of times later on in the expedition when I wished I'd stuck closer to him.

Neck and neck we zigzagged steadily up to the ridge. Colin then drew away from me and I was the last to arrive at the big pile of post office bags above the Surans Ka Dhura pass. The eight high altitude porters including a small wiry man with a green woolly hat called Prataph watched our arrival impassively. They had been sat there for ages no doubt.

We decided that Chris Drinkwater and Titch would do the fixed rope, Andrew, Roly and two porters would traverse and reconnoitre the east facing convex snow slope overshadowed by hanging cornices while Colin and I began digging a path across it. My experience of digging snow paths isn't large. Colin gave me a quick lesson in technique, told me not to overdo it and then struck out across the snow with me belaying him. After sixty metres he cut out a snow bollard, a block of solid snow in the slope, clipped onto it with the rope and a karabiner and so protected us from being swept away by a possible avalanche. Then he advanced another sixty metres and began digging forwards and I began digging towards him.

Digging isn't easy work at the best of times. It's exhausting at 4,500 metres (14,764 feet). One of the porters must have taken pity on me because he started to come out to help but a shout from another cautioned him. That slope was no place to be unprotected. I kept digging and digging, progressing painfully slowly across the slope towards Colin. Titch and Chris Drinkwater watched ready to fix the safety ropes. It was only later that we learnt Titch was feeling absolutely wretched all the while. Time passed and Chris D. offered to swop places with me.

"That's a good idea, Chris. I'm really tired," I said. As I picked my way carefully off the slope Andrew and Roly returned from their exploration chattering loudly about the nerve-wracking snow conditions.

"Bloody hell! Bloody hell! That was scary." Andrew said. "I thought the cornices would collapse any second. I'm not doing that again in a hurry."

"Wow," Roly sighed, flopping down on to his sack. "It's good to be back."

There was a call from Colin. He wanted Chris to belay him so he could see the conditions around the corner of the slope for himself. Confusion reigned momentarily because Chris found it hard to hear the instructions shouted across the snow. The snow bollard belay was removed, then reset and both Colin and Chris finally made it back safely to the haven of the post office sacks and hot chocolate brewed on a hanging stove.

Colin looked up from his mug. "I was wondering about trying to knock those cornices down."

"Have you seen those clouds?" Andrew interrupted abruptly, having looked skywards. We all followed his gaze and saw swirling grey clouds sweeping across the heavens. No time for anything but a hurried re-tagging and re-stacking of the sacks, an about turn and rush to make a rapid descent.

My legs felt a dead weight but it was clear speed was called for. I was bursting to do a wee but "Run down!" was Colin's instruction. So I ran as fast as I could as the wind began to whine and snowflakes stung my face.

"God! Will I make it?" I thought.

At last we could see the tents below and knew that we were out of danger of being caught in the full fury of a mountain storm. We dropped down to the terrace and feeling extremely tired I slowly walked back behind Colin and Chris Smart who'd come to meet him.

"Home Sweet Home" I grinned at her, relieved to be down safe and sound.

* * *

We had a dilemma. There had been an unusually large amount of late snowfall this year. We were now convinced that the Surans Ka Dhura pass was too dangerous to cross during the day with the sun beating down on its cornice topped slope. A night crossing seemed dangerous too. The sugary state of the snow made it difficult to reliably secure fixed ropes for the porters. We were worried. We weren't going to risk anybody's life crossing that slope. What were we going to do?

We decided we'd have to investigate the two other routes into the Siruanch glacier. Titch, Roly, Momoraj, Ranjit and Raju would descend to Malari and try and get a jeep the eight kilometres along the road to Point Eight where a steep-sided gorge gave access to the glacier. This was the low level route that Raju had mentioned. One porter filled us with gloom that evening as he described in vivid detail, via Momoraj, how the gorge had rock falls twenty four hours a day.

Colin, Chris Drinkwater, Andrew, Norbu, Prataph, Chris Smart and myself would form the second party investigating the middle route. This route, the porters assured us, had been damaged by landslides. It was difficult not to recall Roly's dream about the expedition never reaching Base Camp.

* * *

Bed tea was five in the morning. Poor Kalu had either got water from the river, a half an hour's walk down the hillside, or dug away at the ever-decreasing snow patch at the edge of the terrace. Either way it was an arduous business. High altitude mountaineers are neurotic about the necessity of having plentiful clean and hygienic drinking water so as to avoid intestinal complaints and dehydration and we were no exception.

This morning our party set off in the opposite direction to the Surans Ka Dhura pass walking towards the ridge high up above the Girthi Ganga River. Everyone except Chris Smart and I set off at a terrific pace. I soon began to feel quite puffed and fearing that I might not manage to keep up I handed the map I was carrying over to Colin ignoring his hard stare. Chris S., struggling with her stiff knee, was lagging behind me. After some hard walking we eventually came to a tremendous rocky ridge with panoramic mountain views that people in Britain would die for. I looked around and spotted Chris Smart in the distance. I felt a pang for her but my hard mountaineer's heart knew I had to keep up with the others.No one would wait for me and I didn't wait for her. After all I persuaded myself she was Colin's partner, if anyone should wait for her it was Colin. So, having at last managed to catch the others up, I followed them down the plunging sides of the ridge and began what was to be a torturous traverse of an acutely angled slope covered with deep snowdrifts and grasping silver birch trees. It was exquisitely exhausting fighting our way through the tangle of branches and heaving our legs out of snow up to our buttocks. It was for myself, Andrew, Chris Drinkwater and Colin anyway. The high altitude porter Prataph with his green woolly hat and the moustache-stroking Norbu seemed to move through the trees effortlessly.

At last we came to a rock ledge where we sprawled out for a rest, a snack and to consider our progress.

"This route is hell," Andrew muttered. "I'm tired. I don't think it's worth going on. How on earth could the porters get the gear through these trees?" he challenged.

"With bloody great difficulty!" we all agreed.

Andrew and Chris D. decided to turn back and explore a route back to Camp Choping. Colin wanted to continue further to thoroughly check that this middle route wasn't viable. Although far from relishing the prospect of further fights with tree monsters I chose to stick with Colin and we forged forward to a viewpoint where we could see the route was definitely impassable and impossible. Huge rockfalls, probably caused by a major earthquake in the region ten years earlier, had destroyed access to the Siruanch glacier via the middle route. We couldn't get to our Base Camp this way.

"No, it's okay, thanks. I'll hang on to it. It's good for training."

Mad words from a mad woman. I was declining Norbu and Prataph's chivalrous offers to carry my rucksack as they could see that I was struggling on the steep and treacherous journey back across the snow slopes. I was so weary I felt physically sick from the effort of lifting my legs out of the crust-broken snow. A number of times I stumbled precariously on the scree slopes. Once I gasped with irritation, "Just give…a few moments…catch… breath…then I'll…able…do it."

Prataph gave me his hand a couple of times on awkward steps softly saying, "Sister". I hated being so tired but was powerless. "Come on, Ange!" I told myself to no avail until I reached the top of the ridge and could see the green tents far away in the distance but very much there. Norbu and Prataph descended rapidly. Colin kept an eye on me but as we went down I felt so much more energetic I eventually overtook him and walked into camp first. Chris Smart was outside her and Colin's tent reading a book. She looked up as I approached and said, "Where did you get to? I couldn't follow you. I didn't know where you'd gone."

"We dropped down the other side of the ridge," I answered uncomfortably, conscious of feeling guilty at the abandonment. I'd clearly shown no sense of sisterhood. Colin was now nearing the tent. I diplomatically sidled away some considerable distance and tended my soaking wet boots, my sodden socks and wrinkly white feet while some keen words were exchanged.

The high route was impossible. The middle route was impassable. What news would Titch and Roly bring of the low route?

CHAPTER 13
Follow the Road to Point Eight and Turn Right

Well, in fact, just to confuse matters we had to walk to Point Four, four kilometres along the road from Malari, in order to get to Point Eight, which was eight kilometres along the road from Malari. Here's why.

Later that afternoon, much to everybody's delight, the low route reconnoitring team arrived back at camp expressing some optimism about gaining access to the glacier from Point Eight. But logistics were complicated. We couldn't reach Point Eight in one day. The porters would have to ascend all the way up to the Surans Ka Dhura pass early the next morning, collect the stash of equipment and carry it all the way down to some empty barracks belonging to the Border Roads Organisation at Point Four. These barracks would provide a comfortable and convenient camp for the night before we moved onto Point Eight and the Base Camp camping ground early the following morning. Two of the climbing team would have to accompany the porters and retrieve the fixed rope from the cornice threatened snow slope.

It was after dinner that Colin suggested straws should be drawn to decide which two climbers had to slog all the way back up to the high pass with the porters. Much to my relief Colin recognised how shattered I was and I was left out of the cut with Titch. While Titch prepared the straws Andrew kept muttering that he was sure he'd be one of the unlucky ones but he wasn't – poor Colin and Chris Drinkwater picked the short straws. Next morning they were off up the mountain at six thirty following the footsteps of the porters who had left an hour earlier.

The rest of us had a low-key morning sorting and packing gear. Chris Smart and I had volunteered to dismantle our grand earth toilet with its slabs of grey rock as footrests. We then awaited the porters' return. At about eleven we spotted two figures in the distance that we thought were Colin and Chris Drinkwater. All of the heavily laden porters had already arrived at Camp Choping and were now continuing their way down to the barracks at Point Four. They always left us standing – these men of the mountains. Roly, Titch and Andrew had gone down after them. At about eleven forty five Colin and Chris Drinkwater arrived tired but smiling and we were all ready to start walking down to Point Four. As we ambled along Colin appeared in a chatty mood.

"Well, how are you finding things, Ange?" he asked.

"I'm enjoying everything so far, Colin, but then I'm happy to have got to 4500 metres. I don't get as frustrated as some of the others. You know I'm not so committed a mountaineer as they are. I'm just happy being here on an expedition."

We continued down what had become known as Angela's Track moving quickly but carefully as the steep, dusty rock strewn path was frequently hidden under prickly bushes, broken branches, wide-leaved plants and straggly creepers. The beautiful scent of pine lingered in the air and the sun began to beat down. On reaching to grab my water bottle from my pack I discovered that it had fallen out somewhere on the bumpy trip down. Colin and Chris carried on while I about turned, dumped my sack and muttering curses, retraced my steps looking for it.

"Hi, Norbu," I panted near the top of the track. No sooner had I started to explain why I was going in the wrong direction when Norbu pulled out my water bottle from his pocket. Good. About turn and down the track I go again. Norbu and Momoraj soon pulled ahead of me. I tried to keep up as they strode along stepping swiftly over variously shaped and twisted trunks and roots, rocks and boulders but then accepted that they were too fast for me. Behind me some twigs snapped. The tall frame of Chris Drinkwater stepped calmly through the undergrowth.

"Hello, Ange," he smiled when he saw me.

Chris and I walked down Angela's Track together. We took the path left and in due course passed Colin and Chris Smart picnicking under some magnificent towering pine trees. Down we went carefully negotiating the small section of path, which had suffered slippage, passing a small group of Malari men breaking up boulders until at last there were the brown wooden houses of Malari clustered on the hillside below.

Strangely it felt very much like home as I eased myself down next to Chris on the stone bench of the meeting area. There was time to relax before the four-kilometre hike to Point Four. This was alien but known territory. After a little while I took two letters I had stuffed in my trouser pocket down to the storekeeper whom I had been told would give them to a jeep driver to take to Joshimath to forward to Delhi to fly to London to send to Leicester. Norbu and Momoraj emerged from the depths of this general-store-cum-teashop, greeted me and then swung out along the road evidently refreshed. Chris and I followed more slowly discussing our different views of the expedition and its organisation.

Chris Drinkwater has a great deal of experience of going on Scottish mountaineering trips with one or two other mountaineers and being totally self-sufficient. He felt uncomfortable in our set-up, which reminded him of British colonial days, when Indian servants prepared and cooked extravagant meals and waited on Europeans hand and foot.

"I'm used to cooking for myself," he said.

"It doesn't bother me," I replied. "It's through our contact with the Indian staff that we have some access, even if it isn't ideal, to the Indian culture and people with whom we're living. Norbu and Ranjit have enough English to explain things to us."

"Yes, it would be difficult coming over here and trying to organise cooks and porters independently without the language," Chris agreed.

"What's more," I went on as we pushed one foot in front of the other along the dusty road winding above the Girthi Ganga River, "we couldn't manage without the food that they serve up to us. We need the fuel and I don't think we'd have the energy to make it for ourselves in this environment."

As a matter of interest a typical day's meals provided by the cook Yangjor and his assistants while at each Camp would begin with a breakfast of cereal, omelette, pancakes, toast and honey or jam. Tea and biscuits would be at about eleven followed by lunch a couple of hours later which might include deep fried aubergines (eggplants) and chips, puris (deep fried bread) and vegetable curry, red jelly for pudding and cups of tea or coffee. At about four in the afternoon we would have tea and cake. The first course of the evening meal was always some kind of soup followed by four or five dishes including carbohydrates (rice, noodles, pasta and/or chapattis – unleavened wholemeal bread), a dahl (lentil) dish and two vegetable dishes. Dessert could be tinned fruit and jelly, cashew and almond cake, rice pudding or my favourite, egg custard. This was very good living, of course, compared to that of many of the locals but it wasn't roast boar or caviar.

I carried on my argument saying that I thought that everyone of us treated the staff respectfully and that the tidy sum of money that we had paid for their services contributed towards their families' livelihoods. I didn't feel we were exploiting them. I don't think Chris was convinced, although he recognised that he wouldn't have wanted to come on an expedition to India for the first time without the support of an Indian agent and his organisation. Chris and I kept walking in the afternoon sun until at last we saw a group of white painted buildings at the side of the road. As we got closer we spotted the familiar blue and white check shirt of our tea boy, Kalu.

"Namaste, Kalu. Hello, Ranjit!" we called as we passed and within minutes Kalu was following after us with a tray of cool orange drinks. We'd arrived at Point Four.

Unfortunately a porter had made a more spectacular arrival, tripping and then rolling down the extremely steep

Above: Our first view of Tirsuli and Tirsuli West in the distance with Uja Tirche in the foreground. The position of Shambhu Ka Qilla is marked.

Below: 9 p.m. on the 15th May 2001 Andrew, Colin and Angela sort the rope at the start of the climb. We decide to ascend one hundred metres and assess the conditions. (The rest of the team laughed when I read this out to them. They knew we would not turn back!)

(T. Kavanagh)

(A. Philips)

Above: Three sunshine yellow Biblers dwarfed by Shambhu Ka Qilla – the fortress of Shiva. Our route up the south face is marked.

(A. Benham)

Left: Colin in our Bibler tent at Camp 2 below Shambhu Ka Qilla.

(C. Knowles)

The Red Rope Tirsuli North Wall Expedition Team Back Row (Left to Right): Chris Smart, Momoraj Irom, Chris Drinkwater, Tashi Dorjey, Kalu Gurung, Colin Knowles. Front Row: Ranjit Singh, Roly Arnison, Andrew Phillips, Yangjor Tshering, Angela Benham, Titch Kavanagh

(A. Benham)

(C. Drinkwater)

Angela at Camp 1 – 5000 metres above sea level, with Shambhu Ka Qilla and its rock citadel in the background.

(R. Arnison)

Heavy snowfall at Camp Choping c.3800m. A forewarning of difficulties to come.

(A. Benham)

The east-facing slope on the Surans Ka Dhura pass. Colin and Chris D. dig the path that we finally decide is too dangerous to use.

(A. Benham)

The porters and expedition team negotiate the snow covered gorge ascending from Point 8.

Right: Chris climbs the precarious groove of the rock citadel. In his diary he wrote, "It was utterly mad. We shouldn't be here."

(A. Benham)

Above: The North Wall of Tirsuli West. Andrew, Colin, Roly and Titch are on their way back from stashing the first load of gear on the glacier.

(C. Knowles)

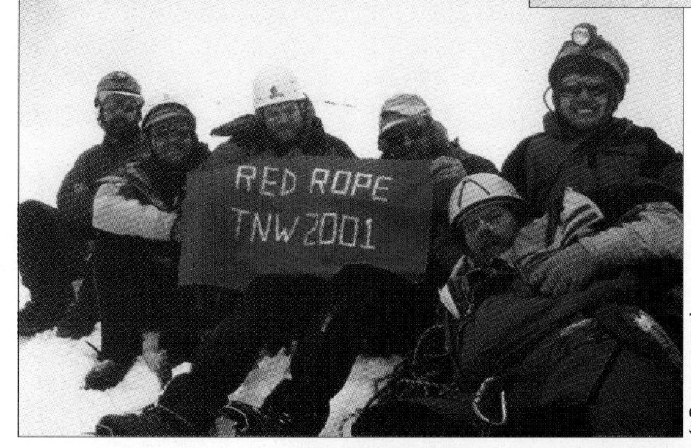

(T. Kavanagh)

Left: The official summit photo. The six of us on top of Shambhu Ka Qilla, approximately 6160 metres high.

(R. Arnison)

Right: Always time for a joke. Roly's summit photo!

(T. Kavanagh)

May 16th 2001. Angela on the summit of Shambhu Ka Qilla – a first ascent and still alive.

(A. Phillips)

The descent. The most dangerous time for mountaineers. After the final abseil Angela slipped and failed to ice brake a little below this point.

Right: After the fall. Angela seated on the slope by the rock barrier, which is thought to have halted her slide. The rest of the team organise the rescue.

(R. Arnison)

(A. Benham)

Time to go home. The last breakfast at Base Camp. Where's Chris Smart? The Indian staff and porters are busy dismantling the tents and sorting the loads.

hillside at the side of the Malari road, the more direct route from Camp Choping. Luckily he escaped with shock, scratches and bruising and declined Colin's suggestion that he might need to see a doctor. Once assured that the porter hadn't been seriously hurt, we turned our attention to the load, which had, of course, rolled with him.

I was dismayed to discover the sack had included some of my gear but fortunately nothing was lost. Colin was less lucky. One of his favourite leather sandals never turned up.

It was approaching late afternoon and all members of the expedition team were lolling about relaxing on the shaded stone porch of the hut where we were bedding down for the night. I carefully patched a tear in my walking trousers and then feeling restless decided to descend the hillside and wash some clothes and myself in the Girthi Ganga River. It was icy cold and spitefully invigorating. How marvellous to be enjoying this wild and beautiful, this so fresh and clear environment. That night I crawled into my sleeping bag on the barracks floor, read a little by candlelight and then fell asleep to the sound of a, so awful it was hilarious, Japanese version of Beatles' hits that Titch had provided for our delight. The next day was my son's seventeenth birthday and we were off to Point Eight.

* * *

By 5 a.m. our camp was on the move. Titch, Roly and Andrew left early to scout ahead. I followed Chris Smart and Colin and Chris Drinkwater brought up the rear. We had four more kilometres march on the stony road alongside the Girthi Ganga, rushing and gushing below us, to a bridge at the Point Eight marker. Here the porters gathered together for a chat and a smoke. They knew that the route ahead would suddenly become a thousand times more arduous than what we'd faced so far and taking their time checked and adjusted their loads in readiness. I was desperate and despite approaching porters dropped down beside the bridge struts for a quick wee. It was just as well I grabbed this opportunity considering the terrain, which confronted us next.

Within a few minutes our motley group of thirty or forty variously attired and burdened individuals began to pick its precarious way across the boulders near the edge of the churning river water. "I would not like to slip now," I thought nervously.

The current was extraordinarily strong. Here was I with my relatively light and compact rucksack. There were the porters; some grizzled old men, some mere boys, almost hidden under enormous weights of gear padding their way in the most tatty and inadequate footwear across the loose scree and slippery stones. But this was nothing compared to what confronted us all when we turned right, away from the noise of the Girthi Ganga. I stopped in my tracks when I set eyes on the 35 degree fiercely steep snow slope that disappeared upwards between a corridor of dark brooding rock and gasped full of awe.

"This is incredible! We all have to go up that," I thought sombrely. In fact I could see a few porters, bent double, high up in the distance. The only way was up so taking a deep breath I set off again. I knew Colin and Chris Smart were some way behind. Chris Drinkwater had caught up and now stepped ahead of me as I toiled on upwards wondering about my sanity.

The surface of the slope was made up of treacherously slippery dirty frozen snow and scattered boulders, which I presumed had smashed their way down from above. I began to feel a little lonely as Chris pulled further and further ahead of me and vaguely attached myself to a band of five or six porters who seemed to be pausing for rests together. After about 500 metres of this laborious ascent we had to turn sharply left off the glacier and make a gruelling rising traverse across a grassy slope that fell dramatically away beneath our feet to the river way, way below. At one point I stood up from resting on the bank of the path and inadvertently kicked a big stone off the edge.

"Oh, no!" I said in horror as the sound of it ricocheting

downwards echoed loudly. "It could kill someone below." Aghast I imagined a porter being struck dead by my dislodged stone. The young porter who seemed to have adopted me appeared quite unperturbed, however. He waved his hand as if to say let's get going, so I put my face forward and carried on, praying unformulated prayers about guardian angels guiding falling missiles so they reeked no havoc.

My feelings of ill-ease were instantly forgotten when I finally pulled myself over the brow of the hillside and could see magnificent views of Uja Tirche and glimpse our goal, a glistening wall of ice garlanded in hanging glacier upon hanging glacier, formidable-looking, even at this great distance. Chris Drinkwater was there to greet me. With an exultant beam he said, "Well, there it is at last, Ange. Tirsuli and the North Wall of Tirsuli West.

CHAPTER 14
Camp Precarious

It was as if the middle-aged porter with the walnut-wrinkled face and the flapping brown trousers and jacket was a Shakespearean thespian playing to us, his audience of grinning porters and bemused mountaineers, in an open air amphitheatre without the indulgence of a decent stage and safety curtain. Behind this ranting performer was a precipitous drop to the river gorge. It was eloquent. It was dramatic but what did it all mean?

It meant that the porters were tired and weary, felt that they had lugged their loads far enough for one day and had gone on a sit-down strike, sitting on a steep grassy slope that disappeared into nothingness although we all knew the river was down there somewhere. Wearily I sat down to watch the pantomime. I didn't like the position. I didn't feel safe. It felt a very precarious spot. For the first time in the expedition I felt seriously unnerved. There was our Polonius porter strutting up and down, shouting and gesticulating, turning as if to walk back to Malari and then striding back to harangue the spectators even more vigorously. I imagined he was saying something like this.

"What are you all sitting there for, you dozy lot of lily-livered layabouts? Let's get back to the thrills and pleasures of Malari and leave this pathetic bunch of foreign limping loonies to sort out their own Base Camp. We've walked far enough. We're tired. We deserve a rest. Raju said our destination was the Siruanch camping ground and here we are hours later on this never-ending traverse, fighting our way through rhododendron bushes and no camp in sight. I say enough is enough. Let's go home!"

Norbu, Andrew and Chris Drinkwater hurriedly consulted. Colin had not joined us yet because he and Chris Smart had waited for Titch and Roly, who were descending from their foray on the snow ridges of Lampak, and had then lost the path. Chris Drinkwater and a couple of porters went ahead some way to see if a more suitable place to camp could be found. Tashi explored the ground above us. All returned reporting no success and the decision was made to dig out terraces for the tents on what became known as Camp Precarious.

When Colin arrived he found the slope littered with sacks, seated porters and expeditioners. The Indian staff were busy digging and levelling the soil, making platforms for the cook tent, our mess tent, a small tent and the gear and using ice axes as tent pegs! He was not pleased. In fact Colin was in a state of white fury. It was obvious that this slope was useless as our final Base Camp. Colin's unavoidable delay had meant decisions had been taken which he would have avoided if he'd been there. He was angry with the boozy Raju, our Head Porter, for not doing his homework properly. Wasn't it his role to explore and scout out the location suitable for a Base Camp? As soon as he had arrived and assessed the situation Colin demanded that Raju go with him to find the path to a suitable Base Camp site.

While Kalu served us tea and biscuits on a tray on this ridiculous slope Colin was discovering the almost ideal Base Campsite a mere half an hour away. Pulling out hair and gnashing of teeth was pointless, however, we were committed to one night at Camp Precarious which was after all wider than many a mountain bivvy ledge.

Our team of seven crammed into the mess tent with mats, sleeping bags and day sacks and tried to get comfortable. We all felt tired and discouraged by the turn of events. Colin's astonishing news that there was what he considered a good campsite nearby was both cheering and frustrating. At least there was a good campsite nearby but what a pity we weren't settling into it this evening.

"Any volunteers to go and check out the campsite with Norbu?" Colin asked. Nobody rushed to answer so I said, "I will, if you like, Colin." In the end it was Chris Drinkwater and I who set off along the track with our head torches in our sacks just in case darkness fell before we got back.

"It'd be a good idea to check out if there's another camping ground even further on," Colin added after describing the route past a rhododendron wood, over a snow bridge and across a difficult step.

"Help!" I screamed silently, "I don't like the sound of this."

Chris and I set off. It was in fact a delightful track that rose and dipped as it followed the winding path of the river far below but dusk was soon to fall and there was a point of anxiety deep in my stomach. We dropped down steeply to the ice bridge, crossed it cautiously, climbed up again and checked our watches. Colin had said it should take us about half an hour to reach the site. Another ten minutes? We negotiated the tricky step over a boulder, walked on a way across a steep grassy slope, rounded a corner and saw stretched out before us this most impressive, wide expanse of abandoned terraces covered in grass and shrub. It was a camping ground. It was a flat camping ground with several independent sources of water running down the hillside behind it about fifty metres above what was now called the Siruanch river. It was heaven compared to Camp Precarious – even though, let's not forget, Tirsuli West was nowhere in sight! We walked across to the far edge, which dropped down to a branch of the riverbed that was covered in frozen snow. Across the drop was another high camping ground with a forest of rhododendron bushes rising up steeply and densely behind it. Little did we realise then what emotions this rhododendron forest would come to evoke in us.

"We'd better go and check that one out," Chris said. I knew he was right but inwardly groaned, knowing time was passing and I was tired.

"You go ahead, Chris. I'll try and follow you. I'm feeling a bit knackered." So Chris was the first to pick his way down, across and up to the rhododendron camping ground. As we had thought there was no water source there and no sign of another camping ground further on. We could confirm that Colin's first choice of Base Camp was good. About turn and back we must go before darkness enveloped us or the threatening storm broke.

We were just in sight of Camp Precarious when the rain started to fall. Dripping wet we fell into the crowded tent as soup was being served. Can you picture rain slashing down, Ranjit emerging from the cook tent, balancing a tureen of minestrone on a tray, slipping and sliding his way across the dangerously muddy slope and offering to dish up through the tent doorway? Of course, we told him we could serve ourselves and to get back to the shelter of the cook tent. Nonetheless it was humbling how we were pampered that terrible evening. Pudding was jelly and cherries.

It was when we sardines were beginning to settle down for the night that Andrew suddenly exclaimed, "Eh, was that a drip?" Everyone anxiously stared up at the tent seams. The rain was pouring down onto the tent fabric. A few minutes passed then. "Oops, there's a drip on my head," Titch said.

"Trust it to be my end of the tent," groaned Andrew. "I won't be able to sleep if this carries on."

I felt a couple of drips on my head now and reassured Andrew that rain was falling on the just and the unjust. Was it Roly who suggested that we could rig up our spare roll of sick pink plastic to waterproof the inside of the tent? Seven bodies began to shuffle and shift about in a very small area pushing and pulling the plastic under the inner tent poles. Then everybody packed themselves down again.

"Aren't you getting into your sleeping bag, Ange?" Colin enquired. I was worried that it would get wet and was considering just sleeping in my clothes. Then the rain stopped and I wriggled awkwardly in trying not to clobber Colin with my elbow. I felt exhausted and mildly gloomy. It was not my best night's sleep but at least I didn't have to confront my fear of the precipitous slope and go to the loo in the night.

The next day dawned bright and cheery. We said goodbye to Camp Precarious and set forth for the Chilkuanch camping ground. This was to be our Base Camp.

CHAPTER 15

Show Me the Way to...the Glacier?!

We had already lost one week going up and down searching and scrabbling about for a viable route to our glacier and ultimately our mountain. Now we had our Base Camp; but at about 3600 metres (11,811 feet) it was far lower than we would have wished and there was no sign of Tirsuli West in the distance. How far away was it?

It seemed reasonable to assume that the way through to the Siruanch glacier would simply involve following the course of the Siruanch River. But how could the six of us manage to transport all the equipment in the time available? We knew that we couldn't. So during the course of that sunny May afternoon, while some of us caught up on washing, chatting, reading and sorting gear, Colin and Momoraj had their heads down with a group of eight high altitude porters negotiating a price for their help in carrying gear up to establish an Advanced Base Camp.

After a lot of haggling a plan and a fee were finally agreed. The following day the porters would have a rest day while we explored the path through to the glacier and stashed some equipment for the next camp. On the following day we would all take up loads. No problem.

Everyone was in good spirits. Roly's dream had not come true. We had established a Base Camp. (Even though Colin was to remind me later it was not the true Base Camp for our route). Here we were in an idyllic spot, restoring our strength for the next stage of the adventure. At the end of our first evening meal at Base Camp, which included an extraordinary iced cashew nut birthday cake in honour of my seventeen-year-old son Max, Colin opened up a discussion on how people in the team were feeling. Andrew was the first to speak. He said that he needed his personal space and was relieved to have the luxury of his own tent now we'd arrived at Base Camp. He admitted to some intense frustration at the delays we had faced in getting this far but hoped progress would now be rapid. Chris Drinkwater spoke next, explaining how he thought that his poor hearing had contributed to him feeling a sense of being on the periphery of the group and he wanted to make an effort to correct this. Andrew said that both Chris and the group had a responsibility to work on this difficulty in practical ways. Chris could help himself by positioning himself in the centre of the group and each of us as individuals could consciously talk more clearly. Everyone could exercise greater sensitivity to the others' feelings. I was struck by what Andrew said and the soft and measured way he said it. This more thoughtful and reflective side of his character had previously escaped my attention. We all murmured our agreement with what Andrew had said and then Roly spoke. He said that like Andrew, he felt, that he was focussed on climbing the mountain. "I'm raring to go, too," said Titch with a broad grin.

"You notice that the two women haven't said anything," Andrew then pointed out and everyone's attention was turned onto Chris and myself.

"I'm fine," said Chris Smart, smiling at the enquiring faces. So it was my turn.

"Well," I said feeling rather self-conscious. "I've enjoyed every day of the expedition so far." (I'd obviously forgotten the previous day's vague depression.)

"Now I'm more concerned about my fitness and strength. I'm desperate that I don't hold you others back or cause you difficulties through my lack of experience." I paused a moment. This was a long speech for me. Looking at Colin I added, "I know I have strengths but I'd want you to tell me if I became a liability."

"You're steady, Ange. That's what I've noticed so far." Chris Drinkwater said reassuringly.

I felt far from steady on several occasions the following day.

* * *

Unlike Andrew, I felt a little lonely in my solitary tent and woke up in the middle of the night feeling breathless and slightly panicky. By four a.m., however, the six of us were up, eating a quick breakfast and finishing packing before setting off along the riverbank. Ranjit, Tashi and Kalu had built a small Hindu shrine to bless our expedition and before we left each of us received from Ranjit, a red mendhi dye mark of blessing on our forehead, to ensure the protection of the mountain gods.

It was a sleepy and subdued company, which found the path down to the snow bridge that gave a convenient start up the river in the direction of the glacier. Unfortunately I managed to misunderstand something Colin said about finding different paths down and while the five of them descended to the right, I looked for a path to the left, which didn't exist, and immediately found myself trailing behind. I had to abandon my route and follow theirs, feeling stupid and cross.

Disconcertingly our handy snow bridge up the river soon gave way to open water, which crashed along at a furious pace. Both sides of the riverbank became increasingly dangerous as we proceeded with steep loose scree, a mass of unstable boulders and slopes of ice sweeping towards the cold grey rushing waters of the river. My pace slowed painfully as I tried to kick steps in the ice with my trekking boots. For some reason, I know not what, some of us had mistakenly agreed that this footwear would be suitable. By this time I was well behind everyone except Chris Drinkwater. "Oh dear," I thought, "it looks like poor Chris gets landed with me again!"

At one point I froze with anxiety halfway across an extremely icy patch and Chris came back to kick steps with his plastic boots. He had been a man of good sense. I was feeling extremely unhappy about the situation and thinking thoughts such as, "This is too scary. I don't want to be here. I want to go back." but I carried on. Going back alone seemed an even scarier option. We both carried on until we caught sight of the others in the distance on some flattish moraine. By the time we reached the spot, however, they had disappeared.

"I'm thinking I might turn back, Chris," I said as we paused to catch our breath. He looked at me.

"Hang on here a bit, Ange. I'll go and see what it looks like ahead."

So Chris strode on a way while I kicked my heels in the ice and moraine feeling distinctly sorry for myself.

"The ground's a lot easier now, Ange. You'll be okay."

We set off again on what was initially much flatter, more solid and friendly ground and I began to relax a little. Then we came to a narrow steep-sided gorge where the murky glacier water was thundering below us and the only way forward seemed to be along the left hand riverbank, a horrible slippery scree slope which moved at every step. I looked down at the churning waters. I knew I could swim but I just wondered what chance my body would have being battered against the rocks by all that wetness.

My foot slipped on a stone. My stomach somersaulted. "I'm not going any further!" I whined. Chris looked back and called calmly, "That's not a very good place to stop, if you're going to stop, Ange." (He told me later that he was beginning to think he might have to dive in and do a rescue.) I was cautiously carrying on a little further, looking for a good place to stop, when all of a sudden there was a shout of "Yoo! Hoo!" from the other side of the bank and there were Titch, Colin and Roly thrashing their way upwards through the undergrowth. They had obviously abandoned the idea of following the river to the glacier. Seeing them retreat, I told Chris more emphatically that I wanted to go back so we retraced our steps to the more secure ground and after a short discussion decided to assault the steep slope on the right of the river where the others seemed to have gone.

It was a relentless and exhausting ascent but the ambience was so much less frightening that I began to feel more cheerful. I noticed the interesting shapes and colours of the band of birch trees we pushed our way through and looked around with wonder at the grandeur of the course the river had cut through the landscape. The next stage of our journey was broken by calls of nature and relief that we were making steady progress traversing an easier-angled but snow-covered hillside. Apparently innocent bands of rhododendron bushes adorned the seemingly endless slopes that we crossed and I began to ask myself the question, "Where is this glacier?"

At long last we saw below us what was without doubt the snout of the Siruanch glacier and way, way in the distance were the others – little black dots moving about on a snow screen. I had never seen a glacier like this before. It was vast with cliffs towering up on both sides sometimes more than one hundred and fifty metres (492 feet) high. As I followed Chris down the rough path slanting steeply to the wide glacier floor three hundred metres (984 feet) below I began to feel a deep sense of foreboding. I was about to enter what seemed a mean and desolate world. The icy heart of the glacier was completely hidden by a layer of shattered rock metres deep, which was in turn largely covered by deep snow. An eerie silence was intermittently disturbed by the cannoning of rock fall, which filled my heart with dread despite choosing a path keeping to the middle of the glacier as much as possible. I was with Chris but as I plodded slowly after him I was conscious of a powerful sense of aloneness and isolation. At one point Chris suggested that he might speed up in an attempt to reach the others. "Okay," I answered, thinking to myself, "Oh, no. Don't do that, Chris." I pushed myself to keep up. On, we plodded, up and down and around the myriad moraine hummocks which made route finding as frustrating as a maze. At long last the magnificent shimmering ice wall of Tirsuli and Tirsuli West came into view far away at the head of the glacier. It was a wonderful and awe inspiring sight. Then we came across the others' footprints in the snow and our spirits lifted.

"We agreed that we'd stop at eleven, didn't we, Chris?" I asked after a while. (This arrangement had been made so that we could return to Base Camp in time to weigh out fifteen kilogram loads for the high altitude porters).

"What's the time now?" It wasn't quite eleven so we continued following the footprints until finally we came to a spot where they turned to the left. It was eleven a.m. This was a good place to stop for lunch.

We sat down on a snow free boulder and scanned the glacier as we munched slices of processed cheese. What a strange place for a picnic in the sun. It was so much more fearsome than the alpine glacier where I'd practised the art of walking like Donald Duck because it helps prevent you tripping over your crampons.

Keen-eyed Chris spotted the small figures in the distance walking towards us so that within an hour the expedition team was re-united and exchanging stories about the various horrendous travails suffered to arrive at this meeting place. The good news was that we could all now head off back to Base Camp together. Some gear had been successfully stashed ready to be picked up next time and carried to Advanced Base Camp. The grim news was that it was still miles up the glacier to Tirsuli West. The closeness of the glinting ice wall was an illusion.

Grim is also how I would describe the journey back to Base Camp and that would be a gross understatement.

What made it so difficult?

We were travelling at midday and the snow kept collapsing beneath us so that we were forced to drag our already tired legs up out of it. The ascent from the glacier up the hillside was cruelly steep. When we arrived near the top of the hillside we needed to find a suitable route back to Base Camp so we split up into groups. Chris Drinkwater and myself found our selves fighting a vicious and unrelenting battle through thigh deep snow and an army of rhododendron bushes that grabbed at your legs, plucked at your eyes and entwined your arms. "Hell is other people"? No, hell is a rhododendron forest that seems to go on forever. Desperately tired and despairing I wondered how I would make it back but what do you do? You go on. There is no other choice and eventually, scratched and torn, we emerged into a clearing and caught sight of the green tents of Base Camp in the distance. We were not home yet but now knew we could make it.

Ranjit and Chris Smart welcomed us some two hours later as, absolutely shattered, we dragged ourselves up the final ascent to the Base Camp terrace. Everybody was in the mess tent gloomily downing tea and biscuits. All our efforts to find a viable path from the glacier had proved fruitless. What in the hell were we going to do?

Colin and Momoraj explained our dilemma to Prataph and our other seven high altitude porters and appealed for their help. In a flash they had disappeared to scour the hillside for a reasonable route from our Base Camp to the descending path to the glacier that we'd found. Within three hours, Prataph returned to confirm that the porters had forged and way marked a path up through the rhododendron forest behind the adjacent camping ground. Although this committed us to a punishing non-stop five hundred metre (1,640 foot) ascent or descent of the hillside every trip we made to and from the glacier it solved our difficulty. The expedition was on again.

I was so weary I could hardly get excited. I was helping pack the porters' loads when Colin suggested that I take a rest so at six in the evening I crept into my tent feeling tired and emotional.

"Is she all right?" I heard Andrew ask Titch whose tent was next door to mine. My answer would have been that I was tired as I had never been before. I was disappointed in my efforts and I was anxious about the task ahead. Dinner was called. As I walked across to the mess tent Andrew asked me directly, "Are you all right, Ange?"

All I said was, "I'm just tired, Andrew. Just tired."

At dinner it was agreed that both Colin and I would remain at Base Camp for rest and recuperation (Colin had pulled a thigh muscle) while Andrew, Titch, Roly and Chris Drinkwater went with the porters to establish Advanced Base Camp. After a lovely meal of tomato soup, rice, paneer (cheese), okra (the vegetable 'ladies' fingers') and jelly for pudding I was beginning to drop off at the table so Andrew sent me to bed. Titch brought water to my tent. I cleaned my teeth and drifted off to sleep with the words of the song "Show me the way to go home. I'm tired and I want to go to bed…" humming around my brain.

CHAPTER 16
Race Against Time

It was four o'clock the following morning when I heard Kalu calling "Bed tea!" outside Titch's tent.

"I'm not going, Kalu," a weak voice called, "I'm ill." A short while later Andrew came over to ask how Titch was.

"Been up all night with my guts, Andy. Can't make it." Andrew wished Titch a speedy recovery and all went quiet again.

Half the team was indisposed. But time stops still for no man and this expedition was definitely pushed for time. However the next two days at Base Camp were spent luxuriating in rest and recuperation regardless of the clock's relentless ticking.

There is without doubt in my opinion some truth in the saying, "No pain. No gain." Would I really have appreciated washing my dirty knickers under the small waterfall behind the Chilkuanch camping ground so much if it hadn't been a blessed relief from tottering on the brink of falling into a huge glacial waterfall? The opportunity to lie and doze listening to sometimes raucous, sometimes exquisitely beautiful music was relished after the grind and pressure of toiling through deep snow and climbing mammoth moraine molehills in a sinister quiet.

Just before midday I heard Colin greet the porters as they arrived back in camp. I looked out of my tent and could just make out the figures of some of the stragglers emerging from the thicket of rhododendrons on the neighbouring camping ground. While the porters ate their lunch of rice and lentils we enjoyed a banquet of chapattis (unleavened wholemeal bread), deep-fried aubergines (eggplants), chickpea curry and salad with pineapple for dessert. Has any meal ever tasted more delicious? I don't think so.

In the middle of the afternoon Momoraj and Ranjit arrived back from the glacier, having accompanied Andrew and the others so that as much equipment as possible could be moved up to Advanced Base Camp. They had had an exciting time finding their way back with Ranjit choosing the river route and Momoraj dicing with death on some wicked scree. A keen ornithologist, Colin had started a nature observation diary, which recorded the many varieties of bird we had seen and heard during our wanderings, as well as the flora. He also mentioned having another rest day. This sounded good to me. I could have set forth the next day but, without doubt, another day of calm and time to rebuild my strength and enthusiasm for the task ahead would prove invaluable. I disregarded the fact that I had sworn in the middle of the trial by rhododendrons that I was never going to leave Base Camp again.

By suppertime Titch was feeling more his normal self. We were all in bed by eight p.m. and looking forward to a second day of glorious relaxation.

Saturday the fifth of May was a true holy day. I had a proper wash – it's amazing what you can do with one small bowl of warm water – and I finished a letter home, which would be carried out by a porter leaving to collect fresh vegetables from Malari.

> *Colin has just announced there are two snow pigeons nesting in an icy crag opposite. We've also seen several Himalayan Griffin vultures...Blue sky, sun shining – feeling refreshed ...salad, vegetable curry and rice for lunch. I must say I fancy a cheese sandwich though... Soon I'll have been away three weeks. Still enjoying*

myself but will be nice to be back.

We lazed about under the mess tent awning chatting with each other about music and Celtic legends, locating Momoraj's district Manipur on the map of India and marvelling at the vastness of the country, reading novels and expedition articles and playing cards.

Colin and I were the keen bridge players. Titch and Momoraj obliged us by agreeing to learn.

It was at dinner that Colin asked if I was going up the glacier next day. "Yes, I'm going up," I said. Titch would be my sole companion as Colin was going to rest his leg another day. I lay down at five past nine that evening, wondering how I would cope with carrying all my gear on what I knew would be a testing journey. Then realising it was four o'clock in the afternoon in England I mused upon what everyone at home was doing.

***

It is only as I've got older that I've come to realise that sometimes I suffer from the inability to recognise the obvious. For instance, I remember teaching how to describe physical appearance to overseas learners of English in the 1980s, using them and myself as models.

"What colour's your hair? It's blonde. "

" What colour's his hair? It's black."

"What colour's her hair? It's ginger."

"What colour's my hair? It's light brown."

The only problem was my hair wasn't light brown. It was a very dark brown. Now it's a very dark brown flecked with white. (As one crag rat noted calling out with a grin one day, "Chalk bag fallen on your head?"). I'll never know how much confusion I caused with hair colours as no one ever challenged me. This would not be the case with the thermals and salopettes saga.

It was that time again – four a.m. in the morning and Kalu was calling, "Bed tea."

I put on my thermals and Paramo salopettes and forced down some rice for breakfast. The packed lunch included the ubiquitous cold boiled potato whose smell made me feel sick so I persuaded Titch to exchange it for his square of processed cheese. By ten past five the two of us were picking our way down to the glacier strip so that we could climb up to the adjacent camping ground, cross it and find our way up through the rhododendron forest on the hill behind. Sweat poured off me as I thrashed my way over logs and through branches on the long ascent in Titch's wake to the lone tree at the top of that unrelenting hill. It had taken us something like an hour and a quarter to be in this elevated position where we could gaze down on our tiny green tents – the first stage of our trek was completed.

"You hot?" Titch enquired looking at my shiny red face. Yes, I was baking hot with my thermals and my salopettes on but I did nothing about it.

The second stage of the trek involved the long traverse across the hill slopes covered in low bushes and snow until we reached the descending path to the glacier. Suddenly Titch spotted some figures by a big boulder below us. Andrew, Roly and Chris Drinkwater were on their way back to Base Camp for some rest, recuperation and decent fresh food. Dehydrated packaged food was all that was available above Base Camp.

Of course we stopped for a chat. We were told that Advanced Base Camp had been established about forty minutes walk up from the previous high point on the glacier. Andrew thought that they had located Chalab, the unclimbed six thousand metre (19,685 foot) peak, which we had identified as an acclimatisation peak or alternative objective if Tirsuli West proved unacceptable. Tirsuli West had looked magnificent but very daunting. It would be maps out and deep discussion back at Base Camp.

Titch and I said goodbye and continued our descent to the glacier snout. So much snow had melted that the scene was almost unrecognisable. What I saw before me now, stretching far away into the distance was a vast expanse of stone rubble, a builders' merchant's heaven and a mountain walker's hell. Hell is other people? Hell is never-ending moraine. On we walked, up and down and around the rock moraine hummocks. A high level of concentration was essential to avoid slipping and spraining an ankle. I was engrossed in watching my feet on the rocks when Titch suddenly called out, "There they are, Ange. There are the tents." I surveyed the moraine eagerly until eventually I made out a tiny patch of green and orange. "Oh, yes. There they are." I agreed. "They're a long way away," I thought. Titch increased his pace while I slowly walked on inching my way closer and closer. The long grind up the ridge to the summit of the Weissmeis, my first 4000 metre (13,123 foot) peak in the Alps, had felt like this. A mountain guide descending with his party had quipped as he passed, "Hope your guide's pulling you hard enough!" At the time I could gladly have murdered the man for the remark. Now the thought of a helping hand was very attractive. However my spirits and my speed finally lifted when I made out, stuck on top of a moraine hummock, a flag – made from Roly's red tee shirt – hoisted on a bamboo pole and flapping vigorously in the breeze.

I dragged myself into the food tent where Titch had settled himself behind the stove and was brewing up some snow water for soup. Morrison's packet mushroom soup with croutons tasted delicious. I spent the rest of the day recovering from the hike. In the afternoon Titch did venture further up the glacier for an hour or so but I remained, reclining on the bumpy surface of the sleep tent reading a book Andrew had left. It was called 'Captain Bligh's Portable Nightmare' and recounted the horrifying tale of the mutiny on the Bounty and the grim and gruesome fight for survival of those set adrift on the ocean by the mutineers. Cheerful stuff, eh? Bligh's rations were worse than ours without doubt but I found the cous cous and mustard sauce we had for tea pretty yucky and I failed miserably at making the chocolate custard thicken. "Ah, well." I wrote in my diary. "In bed by six thirty!!"

The following morning Titch and I took turns bobbing up and down on the ocean waves with Captain Bligh while we waited for Colin to arrive. His white hat was spotted progressing slowly up the moraine just after eleven. Within two hours he'd arrived and was drinking Morrison's soups with us – a troubled man.

"We're still way too far down the glacier," he said, furrowing his brow. "This is more like a lower Advanced Base Camp. We've got to get a camp higher up and soon, too. Time is running out."

The decision was to rise at four next day and move our high altitude Bibler tents, stoves and food as far up the glacier as we could. Colin set off later in the afternoon to do a little recce of the glacier above our camp. I followed when I'd finished Captain Bligh's story but couldn't see Colin anywhere in sight. I presumed he must be a long way ahead of me and to my horror saw in the distance an avalanche crashing down the wall of Tirsuli West onto the glacier below.

"I hope Colin wasn't anywhere near that," I thought.

Dark, pessimistic clouds hovered around my head as I picked my way across the snow and ice and rocks of the glacier. I had never been in an avalanche but the roof of a snow cave had collapsed on me when expedition training in Scotland. Cold, tired and miserable I'd been lying in my old sleeping bag inside the snow cave I'd dug into a snow slope with my companion, when I noticed with disquiet crack lines in the walls. My friend had just assured me that these weren't significant when all of a sudden everything went black. Large slabs of snow and ice had crashed down onto my face. That night was spent with a gaping hole in the snow cave. I didn't sleep at all but perversely felt much happier at the thought of being frozen to death rather than buried alive. I didn't want to die in an avalanche.

I walked on up the glacier noticing how much deeper the snow was here and how many hanging waterfalls of ice flowed and dripped down the glacier walls in the midday sun. They would freeze solid at night. I scaled one of the moraine hills and saw an ice pool on the other side and then more moraine hills but there was no sign of Colin so I turned back. He arrived at Advanced Base Camp not long after me. Yes, he'd seen the avalanche, he said, but it was a long way away from him. We had a lot of walking to do in the morning to get anywhere near the bottom of Tirsuli West.

* * *

It's Tuesday the eighth of May. We set off at five a.m. and it's just getting light. Crunching our way steadily through the crisp snow crust the morning sun begins to shine brilliantly off the north wall of Tirsuli. It glows golden with its bands of hanging glaciers poised to fall. Titch is ahead. Colin is behind and then branches off to the right of the glacier. I wonder about following him but stay with Titch, or try to. Titch strides further and further ahead of me calling out, "Keep your eyes peeled for crevasses." In no time at all I have lost sight of Titch and find myself all alone on the glacier. It is an intrinsically benign glacier I know with just a slight risk of avalanche or hidden crevasses but it feels very lonely. I press on, climbing the jumble of shattered rocks and snow at the edge of deep drops to glassy blue pools of ice. No way could my mountaineering course in the Alps prepare me for this awesome place. How cavalier was my attitude towards crevasses then.

I squirmed as I recalled the crevasse rescue training session on the Trift glacier in Switzerland when a person from each team had to role-play the victim hanging in the crevasse while the other two carried out the rescue procedures. I was the first to play the victim and was told by the guide to jump into the carefully selected crevasse.

"Shall I really jump in?" I queried, meaning should I literally jump in. Taking his look to mean yes, I did a flying leap into the (small) abyss and learnt later that if the guide hadn't been holding the rope as a safety measure I would have plunged to the bottom. How much more cautious I was now.

I knew I didn't want to disappear into a crevasse never to be seen again. "Colin and Titch, no one will know where I am," I muttered aloud.

"Why am I doing this?" I asked myself. "Do I want to?" Never did the quiet predictability of home life seem so attractive. I definitely disliked the idea of an unmarked grave in this desolate spot and miserably placed one foot in front of the other absorbed in morbid thoughts. I was tired and very fed up. Then I spotted two tiny figures in the distance on the other side of the glacier. I thought a moment. There were no other mad fools out on this glacier. It had to be Colin and Titch so I waved frantically to convey the message that I would join them forthwith and gathering up as much energy as I could, scrambled laboriously across the moraine. By the time I arrived there was Colin's rucksack on the snow but no Colin and Titch was eyeing up an enormous black and white streaked block of rock. He was obviously tempted to climb it.

"Hi, Titch," I said casually when I eventually arrived. (Who said I was tired?) "Why don't you climb it?" So up he went. The king of the castle on this massive lump of debris jettisoned on a wide expanse of previously unsullied and unwalked wilderness and what did I have to do? I had to go for a crap.

After I'd taken a couple of photos of Titch in his lordly position, Colin returned.

"Hi, Ange," he said, looking at me carefully. "How long have you been here?"

"Oh, I dunno. About ten minutes."

"Are you totally exhausted?" It would be very hard for me to admit to myself, let alone somebody else, that I was totally exhausted so I replied.

"Well, I've taken some photographs."

"Ah, well, you're obviously not. We've got another hundred metres of vertical ascent until we stash this gear. Okay?"

So off we set again. We passed more rocks and more boulders. I silently laughed between plods when I recalled a friend had told me such lumps had the geological title "erratics." I was an erratic amidst erratics. Plodding on we progressed, self-absorbed, like bowed slaves dragging balls and chain beneath the cruel equanimity of our mountain master Tirsuli which now loomed over us, glaring and indifferent.

Could we never stop?

The ground began to level out and a large lake of iced water appeared on our left. Colin came to a halt and looked around. He glanced at his altimeter watch. We could see the headwall of the glacier some way ahead of us.

"We're at four thousand seven hundred metres," he said. "I think this will do. Let's put up the tents. Here, take this one, Ange."

It was at this temporary camp we called Lakeside that I learnt how to put up our sunshine yellow single skin high-altitude Bibler tents. We levelled the snow, cursed the inside clips which proved irritatingly fiddly and filled dinky yellow bags with snow (these had been sewn up by Chris Smart in England), attached them to the guy ropes and buried them in the snow to ensure extra anchorage in bad weather conditions. Occasionally I had to pause to catch my breath as I panted with the effort of it all. After a brew and a brief lie-down in a Bibler, sheltered from the heat of the now blazing sun, we headed off back down the glacier – Colin's way. This was fractionally less up and down and nerve wracking than Titch's way but nonetheless considerable hard toil in the softening snow. We arrived back at Advanced Base Camp just after one in the afternoon and immediately noticed in the distance a white hat bobbing in and out of sight as its wearer negotiated the twists and turns, the rises and falls of the glacier. Who was it?

It was Roly who staggered into camp half an hour later. Chris Drinkwater, he said, was about an hour behind him. Andrew, struck down by an upset stomach and a sore shoulder, had stayed on at Base Camp. The next couple of hours were spent re-hydrating and erecting another sleep tent, which proved too small for our tall guys and was allocated to the vertically challenged, that is Colin and I. At four thirty p.m. the five of us gathered in the largest tent to discuss the way forward.

Roly opened the meeting by saying how impressed he was by the amount of gear we had managed to shift to Lakeside. I reiterated my concerns about my stamina and my dislike of travelling the glacier alone like Roly and Chris had just done.

"Well, it's a matter of confidence, isn't it, Ange?" Colin responded.

"I don't know, Colin," I continued, "I just don't think I'm going to be climbing Tirsuli West. I don't feel I've got the experience and," I paused, "I want to survive."

Colin made a comparison.

"Look at it this way, Ange, a motorway worker does a very dangerous job but he ensures that he does it as safely as humanly possible. That's what we will be doing." I looked at Colin and then the others but didn't say anything. The fellows decided on a 3 a.m. start. The plan was to carry more food and equipment up to the temporary Lakeside camp, collect the Bibler tents from there and then continue carrying everything up to 5000 metres on the Chalab side of the glacier. This would establish Camp 1 at 5000 metres, assist acclimatisation and provide the opportunity to view the north wall of Tirsuli West more directly.

"Are you up for it, Ange?" Colin asked.

"Yes," I said. It was all very daunting but I didn't want to say no. I slept fairly well that night.

Ah, but what a short night it was. It was the ninth of May, my eldest son's twentieth birthday when I heard Colin's alarm beeping. The difficulty I had that morning getting my disposable contact lenses in my eyes (specially purchased for the trip because I envisaged that they would be easier to use than my usual gas permeable lenses) was excruciating. It was pitch black at three in the morning so I was wearing a head torch that shone in my little hand mirror so that I couldn't see where my eyeball, let alone my pupil, was. Disposable lenses are a lot floppier than gas permeables and every time I thought that I had successfully positioned a lens I drew my finger away to find it folded over in a different place – the back of my thumb, on top of my upper eyelid, on the back of my hand. It was very tiresome and very time consuming, too. Nonetheless I did manage to find my eye enough times to be ready when Colin and Titch were and found myself twiddling my thumbs with them as we waited for Roly and Chris D. At last we set off, a somewhat dozy, ill-tempered bunch straggling across the gloom of the glacier.

"I don't think it's a good idea to wait for each other," Colin called out after slow progress during the first half hour, "we need to get up the glacier while the snow's hard."

We carried on and a little while later I heard Colin muttering and complaining about being left to lead the way when he didn't function well early in the morning. A slight awkwardness hung in the air before Chris took over the lead. Then I took over for a short time. With the coming of light humours improved even though we discovered that we had travelled too far to the right of the glacier and had to circle around to our left to find our little Bibler encampment by the side of the icy lake. We merely paused at Lakeside to dismantle and pack up the tents and the food and stoves that we had stashed there. Then we were off again up the steep ice field which rose steadily on the far left of the glacier.

Gruelling, gruelling was the first section. I felt so weary as I moved painfully slowly towards the others perched on a rock watching my ascent. "Well done," they said encouragingly as I arrived. I wondered if there was some charitable conspiracy concocted to let me go ahead while they sat there because on the second section of the climb up I fared much better finding myself way up in front with Titch. We climbed alongside a semi-frozen stream to an outcrop of rocks adorned with icicles and sat waiting for the others. It was some considerable time before Colin appeared at the brow of the ascent with the words, "Well, it looks like it's we three again." Time passed and then Roly and Chris Drinkwater appeared and sat in the shade of the rocks. The heat from the sun was quite intense now. A discussion ensued concerning our options. We had not quite reached the desired height of five thousand metres. We could wait at these rocks until it got cooler, ascend without the sacks, which we could retrieve later or just carry on. The decision was unanimous, "Let's keep going and get it over with."

The view from Camp 1 at a height of five thousand metres was magnificent. We were directly opposite the formidable 2.5 kilometre soaring North face of Tirsuli West with its complex series of hanging glaciers, steep rock cliffs and buttresses. Titch and I started digging out snow platforms for the tents while Chris set up the stove to make drinks. Behind and above us in the distance stood a mountain with a rock citadel at its peak. I took a photo of Titch labouring away with his shovel with this mountain in the background. We assumed it was Chalab.

While we were shovelling away Colin put up Chris' tent. Roly retired to his tent as soon as he arrived, feeling unwell and absolutely knackered. The sun was beating down on us relentlessly so having drunk several mugs of liquid we all retreated to the relative cool of our sunny yellow Bibler tents. It was siesta time.

It was an hour or two later that I perceived through my dozing and daydreaming that Colin had left the tent for a leak. Then I heard the voices of Titch, Roly and Colin chatting about the prospect of climbing the North Wall. I was all ears when I heard my name mentioned.

"Well, I think Angela might take to that," Colin said. Take to what? "Chalab might appeal."

"Soup's ready!" was called a little later and I crawled out of the tent to see the others grouped round the stove hanging on its tripod of walking poles.

It was while we were sipping our mugs of Morrison's soup that Colin initiated a discussion on what mountain we should climb. We sat facing the proposed objective of our expedition Tirsuli West as the sunlight glinted off its icy façade and the clouds gathered around its shoulders.

"I've given it a lot of thought," Colin began, looking around at us all, "and I've come to the conclusion that Tirsuli West is not for a climber such as me. There are just too many objective dangers. Look at it."

We were in fact all gazing at it, thinking our own thoughts, as another avalanche crashed to the glacier floor.

"There's only one tenuous line up the face that I can make out and that's threatened by seracs and cornices. To climb it successfully you'd need to be so very fast and incredibly lucky. It would be very difficult. I'm really disappointed but I feel that's got to be my decision. It's not for me." Colin paused and looked at us again as we sat there sipping our soup looking at him.

"We have two possible objectives to think about," he continued. "There is the rock-crested mountain behind our camp or Gorur Parvat over there." We looked across at this other mountain that rose up some six thousand five hundred metres (21,325 feet) from the floor of the Siruanch glacier. Another glacier swept down its side separating it from the Tirsuli Wall. Colin said that he could see a route up Gorur Parvat but it would probably take three days to climb and it would be more expensive than Chalab.

"Chalab should prove a more straightforward climb, something like the route we did on the first expedition to CB11," Colin went on, "although we don't yet know what's at the foot of it." He looked around again. "What do you think?"

Titch spoke first. "Well," he said, "this is me as a parent speaking. Tirsuli West is too dangerous. I favour Chalab." There was a moment's silence. Then Chris Drinkwater spoke.

"I'm disappointed about Tirsuli," Chris said, "but Chalab looks interesting. I favour Chalab." I sat there saying nothing and eyes turned to Roly next who sat with his chin in his hand.

"I don't know. I don't know," he repeated shaking his head from side to side. "I'm feeling really confused. I want a decision made but I just can't say. I just can't."

Colin looked at me. "What do you think, Ange?"

I looked down at the snow and said, "I'm thinking I won't climb a mountain but if I were I'd choose Chalab." Chris touched me gently on the shoulder as I said this.

Colin replied looking intently over my head, "I didn't hear the first part of that sentence, Ange, but I did hear the second."

And so followed a brief interlude with Chris asking to be excused while he went for a pee and all of us shifting around while we waited for the conference to resume.

Chris returned to his place in the circle and plans were made. We were becoming increasingly pressurised by the passage of time. Colin believed the porters were due to return to Base Camp on the twentieth of May. Our camp manager Ranjit was expecting them on the nineteenth. We had no more than nine climbing days left however you counted and had yet to be certain which summit we were going to attempt.

"We need you, Chris, and Roly, to recce the approach to Chalab tomorrow morning," Colin said. "We've got to find out if it'll go. If for some reason it won't, we'll need to look at Gorur Parvat and we haven't much time."

That evening four of us walked up towards the rocky-crested mountain we were hoping to conquer. This mass of rock and snow and ice was the focus of our attention now. It stood above us, a little aloof but not totally dismissive, a conical peak surrounded by swirls of shimmering cloud and a deep blue sky. I walked towards it wondering whether I really wanted to climb a mountain, this one or any. I felt hot and weary and was told I was probably over-heating because I persisted in wearing both my thermals and my salopettes. The others descended to the tents while I found a spot to go to the loo. As I crouched, I looked down at the Gorur glacier sweeping between Gorur Parvat and the Tirsuli North Wall. Here was I, a tiny, tiny speck of insignificance in this vast and fierce landscape. It took my breath away.

Colin, Titch and I were getting up very early in the morning to return to Advanced Base Camp and then Base Camp for rest and recuperation and to consult with Momoraj regarding our change of plan. That evening back in our tent Colin and I played one round of knock out whist and three of rummy before settling down for what was to be a long and chilly night. The next day was the tenth of May. We had no time to lose.

The snow was crispy and crunchy as we sped down the ice field from Camp 1 at 5000 metres. I'd heard Colin's watch beep at three a.m. and after a cramped breakfast cooked on a temperamental hanging stove inside the tent, Colin, Titch and I, had bid Roly and Chris "Farewell and good luck with the recce" and set off. We were determined to take advantage of the hard snow crust and were bounding along towards the glacier floor with great vim and vigour when Titch spotted torchlight. It was Andrew's. He had left Base Camp the previous morning hoping to catch up with us but as night had fallen and our footprints had disappeared he'd decided to bivvy under a rock. We were thrilled to see him and explained what Roly and Chris were aiming to do. Then it was "Goodbye and see you soon," and down we went towards Lakeside while Andrew headed up to five thousand metres. The trek down to Advanced Base Camp seemed a little easier than before because the snow was still firm. Titch arrived first and got the stove going for a brew. We had lemon tea and soup and then sorted our gear ready for the next stage of the journey to Base Camp. I packed all my climbing gear and my ice axe in my rucksack because I didn't think it was fair for someone else to have to carry it down if I decided against making a summit attempt. I also thought if it was back at Base Camp with me I wouldn't feel under pressure to return to Advanced Base Camp if I didn't want to. We were just about to leave when Colin said, "Why are you taking your ice axe down, Ange?"

I didn't answer.

"She's not answering me," Colin said to Titch and Titch looked at me.

Feeling on the spot I said, "Do you want me to answer?" They both looked at me so I blurted out, "I'm taking it down because although I haven't decided for certain I think I probably won't climb Chalab." So there it was – out.

"But what are you going to do with yourself at Base

Camp?" Colin said. Images of lazing about listening to music unstressed by moraine and pain began to float before my eyes.

He continued, "And if you do take all your gear down you might as well close the door on the idea of climbing anything because you won't be able to carry it all back up again."

"But it'll save anyone having to carry it down for me if I decide against the climb," I protested.

Implacable Colin continued, "Anyway, Ange, how are you going to keep up with me and Titch if you're carrying all that stuff?"

He paused a moment and then called to Titch, "Do you agree with me, Titch?"

Titch looked at us both and said, "Yeah, I do."

I stood there a few seconds, my mind buzzing and buzzing. "Did I really want to put an end to my summit attempt here and now?" I could not be sure the answer was "Yes" so it had to be "No."

Muttering to myself I pulled the climbing gear out of my sack and stuffed it back into the tent. I unbuckled my ice axe and planted it in the snow trench alongside the others, ready for our return. I swung my now, much lighter, rucksack onto my back and grunting to the others that I was ready we set off down the glacier.

We were not the only travellers that day. To our immense pleasure we came across a snow leopard's paw prints, which stretched out before us showing us the most economical way of negotiating the maze of moraine to the glacier snout. We had a rest at the big boulder and then began the arduous haul up to the traverse path. Eventually we arrived at the lone tree above the rhododendron forest where we could look down onto the tiny green tents far below at Base Camp.

"Get the kettle on!" Titch shouted and figures appeared attracted by the call.Unfortunately we failed to find the true descent path through the rhododendrons and relived our former tussles with branches poking in our eyes, ears and noses. When I emerged from a fight with a particularly awkward and vicious thicket Titch and Colin had disappeared, swallowed up by the bushes, leaving me weary, lost and full of curses.

"I hate you rhododendrons," I seethed as I thrashed the branches aside with my walking poles. "Die! Die! Die!" Until eventually I broke through to the camping ground alive with pretty pink primulas and yellow and black spotted butterflies and saw Colin and Titch patiently seated on a boulder waiting for me to appear.

"Watcha, boys," I called feigning nonchalance. We had yet to descend the steep slope to the glacier and climb up the other side to our camping ground. Titch and Colin stood aside so I could lead the way up the final rough pathway to Base Camp. Ranjit and Momoraj were there waiting for us. I sighed and began the ascent so weary I couldn't think.

"Take the diagonal," Colin called out as he and Titch followed, determined that I should arrive at the top first. Certainly the enthusiasm and warmth of Base Camp's welcome when you return from your sojourn in the wilderness makes a lot of the hardship worthwhile. Ranjit and Momoraj were all smiles and offered help with our bags and Kalu and Tashi rushed out with orange drinks.

One of our conversations on the long journey back had covered what would be the first thing we would do when we got back to Base Camp. I'd said I would eat some of my luxury food – salted cashew nuts. Titch intended to plug in to his mini disc and music. Colin had declared that he would kiss Chris Smart and so he did.

It was good to be back. Could I face leaving this haven for the dark unknown?

CHAPTER 17
All Together for the Final Push

I'm lying down in my tent listening to music. We've had lunch, washed our clothes and lazed around chatting about our hopes and fears. Momoraj dreams of travelling to Venice, Rome and the Alps. He didn't mention Britain, which grieved me a little. Titch spoke of the time that he separated from his long-term partner because, unlike her, he didn't want to settle down and have a family. He left for the Alps but came to realise there that it was feasible to mix children and climbing. They got back together and Titch's painted toenails remain a reminder of his two young girls. I didn't say very much but rather listened. Now I'm here in my tent thinking into my diary and listening to music so superlative it makes me want to weep with pleasure.

Do I want to climb Chalab? I'm tired. I'm worried that it will be too much for me. I'm worried about the pressure of time. I'm concerned about being committed and then finding it's all too much for me. How could it affect the progress of the others I ask myself? I've got to be responsible for myself but am I able to be? So much of the time I'm having to push myself.

It's 8.20 in the evening now and I'm cosy in bed. We've just played scrabble. Both Chris Smart and I queried Colin laying down 'logan' short for loganstone or loganberry but no dictionary handy to check it out – damn it! It was very strange to be sitting above a Himalayan glacier in the middle of nowhere listening to the BBC World Service reporting the

European bank interest cut and General Election news. I wonder how all the folks are back home and fall asleep pondering the question, "To climb or not to climb?"

***

It's Friday the 11th May and I wake up too early, with a stiff neck and an unsettled stomach. Consistency is a consistent problem. A blast of 'The Power of Love' by Frankie Goes To Hollywood and a good breakfast cheers me up a little. Colin and Chris are munching their toast with me when Colin raises the question of what time we should get up next day. I pick up another piece of toast and he continues.

"I hope you climb Chalab, Ange. It's a good first peak. You don't need to worry. The leader will do any technical sections." He pauses and with the glimmer of a smile flickering across his face, serious and intent, adds, "Anyway your gear's all up there."

Hah! I explain to Chris how I'd intended to bring all my gear down so that I didn't feel under an obligation to go and collect it.

"Well, you could say they've done you a favour then. They'll bring it down for you," Chris says simply. Yes, I know that's true.

"I'm worried I won't be able to do it, Colin," I say.

"But at five thousand metres you were snapping at Titch's heels, Ange."

"Yes, I don't quite know how that happened as I had been feeling really tired beforehand."

"The thin boys had probably worn themselves out. You see, Ange, I don't see why you assume that you'll find things any more difficult than the others."

The conversation turned to discussing the tent logistics if Momoraj came up to Advanced Base Camp with us. In theory we only had space to sleep six and Momoraj would make seven if I went.

"Come up with us, Momoraj," Colin said. "The sleeping arrangements can be sorted."

We left the mess tent and went our several ways. I returned to my reflections in the solitude of my tent.

Do I go? I am still tired. In so many ways I'd relish another day to relax and recuperate but time doesn't allow it. It would be nice to be with all the boys and if I don't try I won't ever know if I could do it. And it should be relatively safe. So I think it likely I'll give it a go. GROAN!

In the afternoon we played a boys versus girls game of Trivial Pursuits and three hands of bridge. You need four people to play bridge. Colin and I being the keen and experienced bridge players partnered Titch and Momoraj respectively. It was the first time Momoraj had played but as he carefully worked out the play between his hand and dummy you could see he had the potential to be a good player.

It was over a cup of tea later in the afternoon that I gave Colin my decision.

"I will be coming, Colin," I said. "I'm going to make up the four for bridge."

That night, the night before our departure for the mountain, I again lay in my sleeping bag listening to the beautiful love song of Liu from Puccini's 'Turandot' and yearned for a kiss and a cuddle. I also remembered Ranjit offering to carry my bag up to the ridge because I was a bit slow and wrote with some irritation in my diary, "I am a bit slow I know but I don't really like him saying so. Ah, dear!"

* * *

Yuk! Another hard-boiled egg in the packed lunch. I handed it over to Titch but didn't get the processed cheese in exchange that I hoped for. I was ready in good time. It was three thirty a.m. and Colin and Titch were just fastening their sacks. We walked over to where Momoraj seemed to be in a fluster with his packing.

"Could you put this mug and spoon in my rucksack, please, Angela," he said and I found a space with some difficulty in his full to bursting sack. It towered worryingly above him when he finally swung it onto his back. Off down the path to the glacier across to the adjacent camping ground we went. Momoraj was hindered by having a hand torch instead of a head torch and lagged a little way behind. I was keen to keep in touch with Titch and Colin who were setting a brisk pace. Down we went to the glacier, then up steeply on the other side, placing our feet as carefully as we could on the loose, stony hillside. All of a sudden a rock went flying past me and I heard a thud. A groan echoed in space and I turned to peer into the darkness.

"Are you okay, Momoraj?" I called down anxiously. There was a muffled response.

"A rock just hit my knee."

I paused wondering what to do, but when I heard footsteps, I again continued plodding on upwards. Then after a few minutes Momoraj shouted up to me, "I'm going back. My knees are hurting. I'll come later."

I heard Momoraj turn around and start descending. Plodding on and on upwards, I laughed wryly at the irony of it all. Here was my bridge partner deserting me. I needn't have decided to climb the mountain after all!

***

It took us one hour and five minutes to find our way up through the rhododendron jungle to the lone tree. We pressed on along the traverse and then dropped down to the now familiar glacier snout. Then the hard grind up the glacial moraine began with me forever in the rear. Periodically Colin and Titch would stop and I would catch them up.Then we were off again and I found myself trailing behind once more. My mind drifted back to the first-aid course we'd completed just before leaving for India. After the embarrassment of 'killing' Colin in the role-play in the morning and having my head filled with facts about high altitude afflictions – pulmonary oedema, hypothermia, frostbite and flatus expulsion in the afternoon, I felt like a break and decided to go for a run with Andrew around the local park. I forgot he was ten years younger and a half marathon runner and trailed behind him the whole way. This was it. I was just not as fast as these men. I couldn't keep up but I kept on going, mumbling and moaning to myself about glacial moraine, hell and never-ending torture. In due course I was moving my limbs in a trance of exhaustion, which was suddenly shattered by a noise ahead of me. There was Titch in the distance waving at me and there, to my huge delight, was Roly's ragged red tee-shirt flag marking the site of Advanced Base Camp. I felt a million times better. I walked into camp and saw Andrew's face peering out of his tent, "What you doing in there, you lazy bastard?" I called happily. We were all together again.

The next few hours were spent sweltering in the beating heat of the Himalayan sun. Andrew hadn't been as lazy as I'd imagined. Overnight he, Chris and Roly had carried a load of gear up to Camp 1 and were now back at Advanced Base Camp taking a well-deserved rest. Throughout the expedition we'd aimed to climb high and sleep low in an effort to assist acclimatisation to the lack of oxygen at higher altitude. In fact our frustrating difficulty in establishing a route into the Siruanch glacier did ultimately help us avoid high altitude mountain sickness completely.

"Sorrrrrrrry!" I chirruped to the boys when I realised how I'd misjudged them. This time I had no book to read and time sidled by as we flopped and dozed the hot, stuffy hours away. Tea was Smash mashed potatoes, mushroom sauce and anti-diarrhoea tablets for me, stricken again by the dreaded Himalayan gut. I didn't even fancy the treat of my childhood, chocolate Angel Delight pudding, which the fellas had whipped up to celebrate our arrival at Advanced Base Camp.

We'd agreed to leave for Camp 1 that night so we could make speedy progress on hard snow and at ten p.m. were up and ready to go. Initially we stuck close together but as time went on and we approached the temporary Lakeside stash I began to feel more and more exhausted and dropped further and further behind. I thought that I'd passed the big black boulder, which Titch had stood on that first foray up to Lakeside, and that soon I'd meet up with all the others and we'd regroup but there was no sign of them. I couldn't stop myself muttering and moaning querulously to Chris Drinkwater, who'd kept with me, "Where the bloody hell are they?"

Eventually we met Titch waiting for us who, on seeing that Chris and I were together, said he was cold and would get on and instantly disappeared into the distance. I groaned with tiredness and bitter rage and feeling absolutely wretched plodded on, occasionally spotting a flash of tantalising head torchlight ahead. I hated everybody and everything in the world as I toiled up the ice slope behind Chris. When we reached the ice stream, where we'd previously stopped by the icicles during my brief moment of walking triumph – silver behind Titch's gold – Chris told me that there was one more steep rise and then we'd be there. I staggered on upwards at a crippled snail's pace and upon reaching the top of the rise looked frantically around. I couldn't see any tents.

"Where are the Biblers? Have they moved them?" I panted out desperately.

"I was lying," Chris said flatly. "There's one more slope to go. I think I saw Colin wave."

GROAN! I staggered slowly on for what seemed like hours and hours until at last there indeed were the Biblers and a voice echoed from within one tent, "Throw in your sleeping bag and karrimat and come in, Ange."

At six thirty in the morning I crawled into my sleeping bag a weary, wretched and disheartened woman. Misery and gloom hung over me.

This was it. This was what I'd been worried about. Here was I – so slow, lacking energy, no stamina. Shattered and weepy I slunk in my sleeping bag sniffling into my silk liner. Time passed. The sun shone brightly on the Bibler but I kept my head buried, full of woe, until Colin asked, "How is the inner Angela?"

I told him how shattered I felt and that my poor performance last night was what I'd feared might happen.

"My silk sleeping bag makes a good hankie though, Colin," I joked weakly.

"You'll have to turn it round so it doesn't crackle too much, Ange," he replied and reminded me of the time I'd been ahead with Titch.

That morning I spent dozing and sleeping and drinking hot drinks prepared by Colin – cherished I was, and by the afternoon I felt a fair bit better. We planned to move up and establish Camp 2 at ten that evening. There was last minute sorting of the food supplies and decisions about who carried what and risqué photos taken of team members pottering around Camp 1 in their underwear, some rounds of whist, a doze and then it was ten o'clock and departure time.

I followed behind Roly with Titch and Colin in the rear. Andrew and Chris followed a little later. We had to ascend a steep ice slope to the upper glacier. I managed this quite strongly, despite the snow being difficult, but at the top began to flag. Titch and Roly ploughed ahead looking for a suitable spot to pitch camp. Colin and I walked along the glacier together. I felt tired now and wanted to reach the destination immediately. The site was eventually chosen and we all set about pitching the tents. I didn't like the look of the snow heavy glacier walls and ensured that my and Colin's tent was pitched the furthest away from them. Then we all disappeared into our sleeping bags and didn't emerge until mid-morning.

* * *

How do you spend the day on a Himalayan glacier at some five thousand four hundred metres (17,716 feet)? You heat countless pans of snow in a pan over a stove hanging from a tripod of walking poles and make mugs of hot chocolate and lemon tea – in between cursing the cheap Indian lighters for not lighting. You chat about this and that –

the wish to break out of the rut of your career and do something new, the problems associated with being a bit of a perfectionist and possessing an underlying lack of confidence. Colin suggested that I underrated myself as a member of the expedition team, failing to recognise that I had something to offer to the team, but I didn't agree with him. I felt that I recognised the strengths that I had and was willing to give my opinion when I felt qualified but that in most circumstances on the mountain I was hindered by my lack of experience and knowledge. I did, for instance, feel quite confident in my ability to interact positively with people belonging to a different culture and background and had demonstrated this during the trip.

Early that Monday afternoon we had a meeting – all six of us crammed into Andrew and Chris' Bibler tent (quite a feat). It was decided that Titch, Roly and Andrew would go back down to Camp 1 to collect the rest of the climbing gear while Chris, Colin and I did a recce of possible routes up the mountain. I was relieved and grateful that the boys were willing and able to do another carry and a little amused at the notion of me contributing to a discussion on the best route up the South face of our mountain. There was some talk of attempting the attractive looking East ridge but the general feeling was that it would take more time and time was what we lacked.

At four p.m. Colin, Chris and I set off across the glacier to study the different gullies at the base of the mountain.

"We need to look at each one in turn," Colin said as we tramped across the snow. He smiled, "It would be self-indulgent of me to go to my favoured one first."

A large icy lake was discovered below the first gully, which made accessing it very difficult. It was also unsuitable because of the known danger of rock fall. "I saw rocks ricocheting down there earlier this afternoon," Colin murmured to Chris and I. We walked along the base of the mountain to gully number two. This was the favoured one. I stared up at it as Colin explained his route up the gully to a buttress where you had to trend right up to another buttress and then on to another and so on until you approached the snow slope below the rocky citadel. Here you had to move right to the citadel's base.

"Oh, as simple as that?" I thought to myself. Initially it was as if Colin was talking complete gobbledy gook but as I studied the face more intently I began to see the logic of the route upwards.

We walked on to look at gullies three and four but agreed that both featured much more technically difficult rock climbing problems than gully two. It was decided. We'd ascend a snow slope at right angles to the mountain so that we could gain a better sense of the angle of the snow ramps above gully two. To get to this steep slope we had to descend a deep snow bank by the side of avalanche debris that had fallen on to the glacier from huge cornices hanging from the bounding cliffs to our right. I looked at the cornices anxiously as we sunk to our thighs in the soft snow. The weather was changing. The sky had darkened to a steely grey and flakes of snow were beginning to blow about. Having descended we then had to climb.

"Use the shaft of your axe," Colin called, reminding me that although a steeply angled slope it was not acute enough to warrant using the pick of the axe. Chris Drinkwater forged ahead with Colin behind and myself following slowly and tentatively. I reached five thousand five hundred metres, a little below the two men, who checked out the condition of the rock and concluded it was incredibly brittle. On the descent Colin explained that the snow slope I had just gone up was about the grade that we'd meet on the mountain.

"It's about grade one or two, Ange. No more than what you've done on Hidden Gully in Wales." I remembered that trip – my first ice-climb in North Wales. Colin had rung at short notice saying ice-climbing conditions were forecast. Was I ready? Of course I was – once I'd rushed off to the gear shop to buy the ice hammer I needed.

"The slopes up there are certainly no more difficult than

Central Trinity," Chris added encouragingly. He and I had done this classic Snowdonian route earlier in the year.

"What about the Citadel, Colin? What grade's that?"

"Ah, well, that we don't know, Ange, until we get there," Colin said.

Now the snow began to fall heavily, driving into our faces and stinging our eyes as we battled our way back to the tents, which had almost disappeared in the blizzard fog. By 7.30 p.m. however, the snow had eased and Titch, Andrew and Roly were able to set off back down to Camp 1 to collect the remaining gear. I didn't envy them.

It was my turn to cook the supper and the core-chilling, slow, tedious process of snow melting began with me setting up the tripod of poles outside the Bibler. Cooking outside was a cold, miserable, lonely affair – a mistake. Next day we melted snow on the gas stove hanging inside the tent where it was much warmer, relatively cosy and more companionable.

The soup I made that evening was lukewarm. The noodles and cheese sauce were hot and tasty according to Colin but, gagging at every mouthful, I had to force them down me knowing that fuel was vital for the climb ahead. As for the semolina for pudding – that was a major disappointment. It stuck to the pan and lacked the particular delicate taste that I remembered from schooldays. Brrrrr...It was cold and wretched on that glacier that night in the middle of eternity.

* * *

Gloves, gloves, gloves. Gloves, gloves, gloves. I lay in my sleeping bag and a vision of all manner of gloves kept visiting me as I desperately tried to sleep. There were big black Goretex gloves and thick woollen Dachstein gloves, small thin Thinsulate gloves and bulky leather ice axe gloves. I had brought six pairs of gloves on the expedition with me but for some unaccountable reason I'd decided to leave three pairs at Base Camp. As I lay tossing and turning in my sleeping bag through the long hours of night I felt a horrible worry in my bowels that the gloves that I'd chosen to bring for the summit attempt were inadequate. I woke up the morning of Tuesday the fifteenth of May with an aching head and a feeling of nausea.

"Why don't you take something if you feel sick?" Colin suggested. I did, and then trudged off across the glacier, under the overcast sky, to the loo hole behind a boulder. I felt awful. Cooking outside in the cold had done me no favours. We took the stove inside and brewed sweet warming drinks while it snowed steadily outside. Later on Colin halted another trek out into the cold saying, "Why don't you wee out the back end of the tent while I wee out the front?" As the day went on I began to feel better both physically and mentally though the weather was far from encouraging. It continued to snow and the occasional avalanche could be heard in the distance. Little noise came from Titch and Roly in the far tent but a steady stream of moans and curses emerged from Chris and Andrew's. The unreliability of the Indian lighters was sorely trying Andrew's patience.

The anguished cry "I'm just sick of these bloody things," echoed across the glacier basin more than a few times.

A meeting was necessary to discuss the way forward so at 11 a.m. we all squashed into Chris and Andrew's tent once more. The question was whether we were going to climb this day or wait until the next – the last day possible to climb. The timing was extremely tight. The atmosphere in the tent was serious and subdued as Colin put the question to each of us in turn 'to climb or not to climb' that evening. There was concern that the weather would worsen the following day and put paid to any attempt on the summit. There were anxieties about the snow being unsafe. At the same time there was almost an eagerness to get the climb over and done with after weeks of planning and anticipation. Roly talked about a feeling of 'cabin fever' following a morning of being cooped up in the tent. Finally we decided that we would meet at 4 p.m. to get the gear sorted for the climbing teams. The two teams would include a main leader, Colin or Titch, a specialist leader, Andrew or Chris and myself and Roly. Whereas Titch, Chris and Roly would climb conventionally on two ropes, in recognition of my lack of experience Colin would lead from the middle of one rope with Andrew and myself tied on at each end. This way Andrew could climb alongside me much of the time offering support and encouragement. We returned to our tents to wait.

That afternoon could have been long and tedious but Colin and I spent much of it sticking strips of silver gaffer tape on to a large oblong piece of silky red material so that it spelt out Red Rope TNW (Tirsuli North Wall) 2001. This was to be our summit banner. Hopes were high despite the snow flying about outside on the glacier.

The hours passed. It was four o'clock but so much snow was falling the gear sorting was postponed for half an hour. Then four of us crawled out of our tents and began to jingle and jangle as we sorted out slings and karabiners, ice screws and pegs. The fact that Titch and Roly remained tucked up in their tent while Chris selected the gear for their team caused Colin some irritation. When Chris then walked off with the screws and pegs, which had been put in our pile of gear, there was some vehement, under the breath, muttering about people not bloody listening. Tension was in the air.

Back to the tents we retreated to prepare water bottles and force down a last meal before departure.

"Are you feeling apprehensive?" Colin asked as I poked at the snow melting slowly in the hanging stove.

"Yes, I am," I answered with no hesitation, "but I'd rather be getting on with it than hanging around here any longer. What about you?"

"I always get apprehensive at the start of any climb," Colin replied quietly.

At seven fifteen Colin settled down to sleep. I said that I would wake him up at half past eight and dozed fitfully, looking at my watch anxiously every ten minutes or so. At one point I sat bolt upright in the tent realising that I'd almost dropped off completely. It was eight twenty five p.m.

I remembered watching Colin earlier in the day walking towards our gully, counting paces so that we could find it easily at night.

"It's half past eight, Colin. Time to get up."

Our team was ready first. It was snowing lightly but there was no wind. We set off across the dark glacier at nine p.m. snowflakes blowing in our faces. It seemed a long, long trudge in the dark. At the bottom of the gully words were exchanged.

"Well, what do you think? Is it on or not?" one said.

There was a pause and then the reply came. "Let's go up a hundred metres and see how it looks there."

CHAPTER 18
Summit Day

Summit Day – Wednesday 16 May 2001. This was the day that was nearly my last.

I had accepted the challenge of climbing this mountain and had to see it through. There was no turning back. It was terrifying.

The spindrift stopped flowing down the mountainside onto us and we all breathed again. It wasn't an avalanche. Then we pulled our hands out of their white burial mounds and tried to shake them back to life.

Our six head torches resumed their slow march up the South face. "You're doing well, Ange," Andrew encouraged me as we toiled on upwards. I cursed myself for not bringing better gloves.

We carried on up under a now lightening sky. Conditions weren't easy. It was still snowing and my hands were getting increasingly cold.

But progress to below the citadel was relatively fast. Colin discovered with some relief that he'd done an excellent job of route finding in the dark. By six in the morning we were all huddled on belays as, bathed in watery light, he led up towards the steep parallel grooves at the citadel's eastern end. The wind was icy and chilled you to the quick. I wriggled my fingers, desperately trying to keep them warm in my frozen gloves.

Colin's lead across to the citadel grooves was slow, arduous and fearsomely exposed. A number of times we heard him cursing the poverty of the snow as it collapsed beneath his feet. Into the groove he disappeared and we waited and waited in the biting wind under a now bright blue sky.

At long last the word, "Climb!" echoed down to us and Andrew and I set off upwards kicking steps and banging in our ice tools. Having reached the rocky ledge where Colin had established himself at the base of the citadel, Andrew chivvied me to help sort out the anchors for the belay.

"Come on, Ange, you can't be carried, you know. You've got to make yourself safe as you would on an ordinary rock climb."

"Yes, yes." I thought. "I know. Come on brain. Get working."

Once safely belayed in the groove I took off my gloves and inspected my right hand. Colin and Andrew saw the telltale signs of frostbite – the tips of my two right middle fingers were white and waxy.

"Suck them, Ange. Suck them," Colin urged me before leaving to lead the next pitch. "You've got to try and get the circulation going again."

So I sucked them and I blew on them as Colin led the first pitch up the groove on what he found to be poor rock, poor snow, poor ice and poor protection. Later discussion was to conclude that the grading of the pitch was the top end of Scottish grade four – an ambitious grade to be climbing above six thousand metres apparently. Of course, at the time I was blissfully unaware of this, standing there sucking my fingers like a baby, waiting for the command to climb. And it came, echoing eerily down the groove.

Off I set with Andrew behind me, kicking in my crampon points, swinging and placing the picks of my ice axe and hammer as effectively as I could, and heaving myself upwards. Slivers of ice and splinters of rock shot here and there. Occasionally the picks jumped out of their placements and I balanced precariously on my front points as I reached and swung for a sounder patch of ice or a niche in the rock.

My only thought was to keep going. I had no other option but to reach for the sky. At last Colin came into view and I felt a sense of relief that I might actually reach him. What did I say as I climbed onto his belay ledge? Something inane no doubt such as "Hello, Colin. Here I am."

Andrew climbed up onto the ledge beside me. "Wow," he said, grimacing and grinning at Colin.

"Looks like the final pitch," Colin responded nodding upwards. "You take it."

"You sure, Col?" Andrew looked up to the jumble of rocks at the base of the next groove.

"Yep, I'm knackered. You do it," Colin repeated and Andrew began to sort out the gear for his climb. Away went Andrew, murmuring and muttering to himself in his usual fashion as he tried to find a way through the rocks and ice to the summit groove. Eventually he got himself established in this second groove and we were left with the sound of ice picks cracking into ice and rock.

"Grade one or two climbing, Colin," I said wryly to Colin belaying at my side. "I don't think so." I was vaguely aware of feeling that it was all much harder than I wanted. Yes, I was committed but was this really what I wanted, was this where I wanted to be? Maybe the answer was yes – if I survived – but if I didn't...

"I said I didn't know what grade the citadel was," Colin replied.

Suddenly down below us, we heard the sound of scraping crampons, ice axe and hammer ringing loudly as they struck and splintered rock and ice. Chris Drinkwater's white helmet came into sight and we heard him cursing and swearing with each blow of the ice tools.

"This is bloody ludicrous," he shouted.

"Watch him, Ange. Watch him," Colin told me. "Chris is the best technical ice-climber amongst us."

"Good God," I thought, "he's the best ice-climber amongst us and he's calling that pitch ludicrously difficult!"

Meanwhile Andrew was nearing the summit and our

attention was diverted from Chris by Andrew's loud gasping shouts of, "Wow, this is wonderful. Just wonderful."

He'd reached the top.

I was to go up second. Chris Drinkwater felt too tired to lead another pitch so he came up behind me and Colin followed behind him with Titch and Roly's rope tied on the back of his harness.

The last pitch was challenging again but I bashed my way up with a fair amount of energy. The only way was up so there was no point hanging about – Bash! Bang! Bash! went my ice axe and ice hammer. The last pull up onto the summit was tricky. There was Andrew sitting in the snow looking down at me.

"Come on, Ange. Almost there."

I pulled and I kicked and slithered in my ungainly walrus fashion onto my first Himalayan summit.

What an anticlimax! Was this the top? There was another peak that seemed just a stone's throw away from us.

"I'm not bloody well going up there as well," I thought angrily. "Please don't let anyone say we're going up there as well."

"Well, here we are on the summit," said Andrew as one after another we hauled ourselves onto the three metre wide top. "But it ain't Chalab."

It isn't Chalab. What on earth is he talking about? Don't tell me that peak over there is Chalab. Oh, God. Surely we're not going to climb that as well.

In fact I learnt later that our nameless peak had twin tops, which were about thirty metres apart and of similar height – about 6160 metres – and nobody planned to ascend the second top. The mountain was not Chalab, the peak that we thought we were climbing and whose whereabouts was, and is, something of a puzzle and a mystery. I learnt following this experience that it's not so uncommon for mountaineers to find themselves at the top of the 'wrong' mountain!

Now that the four of us were on the summit, I saw Colin and Andrew indicate to Chris that he should belay Titch and Roly. I felt so sorry for Chris as he wearily sank down onto the snow with the belay device in his lap. He seemed utterly exhausted, sat there slouched over the rope. Two pitches below Titch and Roly waited, a little confused by the delay but eventually realising from the tugs on the rope that it was now safe to climb. Titch began his ascent. While he was working his way up the 'ludicrous' groove, Colin was sullying the virgin white snows of this unnamed peak by having 'a dump' as he coined it. My aesthetic sense couldn't help but wish he didn't need to answer a call of nature although there was no doubt that this release was well deserved after the tensions of the climb.

Andrew got out his packed lunch and lounged back on a rock on a snowy platform a step below the summit and I sat beside Chris eating a supposedly cocoa-flavoured energy food called Peronin which I thought tasted more like Bovril. Mist and cloud had closed in now and I failed to make out Nanda Devi in the far distance as Colin had done.

At long last Titch's head appeared above the groove and he climbed up beside us grinning broadly. "That was fun," he said and almost immediately started taking photographs of the views. The Tirsuli North Wall drifted in and out of cloud and Dunaghiri was just visible over the top of the Gorur glacier. Spurred on by Titch's example I took a couple of shots but aware that the most important part of summitting a mountain is surviving the descent, felt too anxious to take many. Titch was now eating and burping loudly as is his wont. Chris seemed in a complete daze as he belayed and I began to feel a little concerned about the length of time it was taking Roly to reach us.

"Are you okay?" I shouted down the groove.

Eventually Roly's head popped up and he dragged himself onto the summit beside us. He was okay, just extremely tired.

We were all up. It was now time for the summit photograph but whose camera should we use? Exhaustion and altitude has a debilitating effect on your powers of reason and decision taking and it took some discussion to conclude Titch's camera would bear the responsibility of recording our first ascent of this virgin mountain for posterity.

The topic of the next discussion was how to get down.

Colin, Titch and Andrew considered the options. A good ice screw placement was possible but how could it be effectively backed up. The snow quality was too poor for a reliable snow bollard, a horseshoe block of snow cut into a snow slope, and there were no decent rock placements. Eventually the decision was made that a fairly big boulder would make an adequate backup for the ice screw and Colin prepared to abseil down. The protocol was, I discovered, that those without family responsibilities took the most dangerous first and last positions on the abseils. Having agreed the code for which rope to pull down was "pull-yellow", Colin disappeared over the top and down. The ice screw held. I was keen to get going and went second, having asked Titch to check I had set my gear up correctly and see me over the edge.

Down I went for sixty metres. Chris Drinkwater followed me while Colin set up the second abseil. At the bottom of abseil number two we had a long and cold delay on a snowy ledge. Then when we reached the bottom of abseil number three the weather started to deteriorate and it was clear that Colin was finding it difficult to find suitable anchors for abseil four. I sat crouched in the snow with Chris by my side watching the billowing clouds sweeping in around us. The wind was bitterly bitter and the greying sky bleak.

"Things look grim," I muttered pessimistically to Chris. "I don't like the look of this." Chris said nothing and I continued to stare gloomily at the play of nature before our eyes. I seriously wondered what our chances were of getting down alive. Gloom and doom filled my being. Roly was waiting on the ledge above us trying to shelter from the chill air. How many minutes, hours, days did we wait there? It seemed like an ice age. Then Colin gave us the call and we descended to where he'd been struggling to set up the next abseil safely.

We all descended to this abseil point until there were six of us in a cluster and Titch was asked to test the snow bollard Colin had painstakingly dug out. Slowly Titch leant back on the rope and instantly the snow bollard disintegrated. What was the next move?

After a short discussion Colin agreed to cross to a rocky ridge and look for peg placements there. Carefully he crossed the deep, unstable snow. At one point this collapsed beneath him, making him yelp out, "Oh, my testicle!" No bollocks from our leader note! The five of us watched intently as Colin fiddled and levered and clanged and banged the pegs and rock. At last he stuck his thumbs up to show he had found a placement and we traversed across to him one by one.

Abseil number four consisted of four pegs placed in a row, which disconcertingly bent when weight was put on them. Everyone's eyes stayed riveted on these pegs as the person in front descended.

Colin, Titch, Chris and I used a single rope for the final abseil number five, which took us to the top of a long, steep snow gully. There we unclipped from the abseil rope and unroped started to descend at our own pace using our ice tools as necessary. I proceeded quite slowly and soon lost sight of Colin, Chris and Titch as they hurried downwards but I could see Roly and Andrew above me as I descended facing in to the slope. They had doubled the ropes to abseil so that they could be retrieved and were now faced with the task of coiling them and packing them away.

"I like the way they bloody well leave us to sort out all the fucking ropes," Andrew complained petulantly to Roly. He was not a happy bunny. He was livid. Dropping his glove on the snow slope was the last straw.

"Bloody hell! Glove below!" he shouted to me hoping I would catch it – but it went whizzing past before I had a chance to grab it.

So I continued downwards aware that those in front were out of sight and Andrew and Roly were now moving swiftly, and were going to pass me soon. I didn't like it. The rational part of me knew that it wouldn't happen but I was worried I would be left behind. As Andrew passed me he said, "You can use your ice tools to help you slide down." So I started to move more quickly. Roly passed me and I tried to descend even more quickly so as to keep up. Then all of a sudden I found myself moving much faster than I had bargained for. I had lost my footing, failed to get the ice tools to bite the ice and before I knew it was sliding out of control down the slope.

Past Roly I slid. He called out to Andrew. Andrew moved to help me but got into a slide himself and had to do an ice axe arrest. On the third attempt he managed to halt his slide. I whizzed past.

I remember passing a blur, which was Andrew, and registering his shout of "Brake, Angela! Brake! Use your ice axe."

But that's easier said than done when a slip has become a full-bloodied s-l –i- d-e. I had practised ice axe braking falling on my front, falling on my back and falling headfirst but I had never tried it while holding an ice tool in each hand – the lesson on 'How to self-arrest without getting an ice pick in the brain.'

I try to get hold of one of the ice tools flailing around at my side. I touch the handle but no way can I get a grip on it, get on top of it and get it to bite into the ice.

I feel myself in free fall and questions flash through my brain, "When am I going to stop? Am I going to stop? Will I feel myself fly into space?"

I don't see the sparks fly as ice axe and ice hammer crash against the rocks or feel my body bounce as it tumbles and rolls crazily past Colin and Chris.

Colin considers trying to stop my downward plunge but realises that could cause more harm than good. Chris believes that the fall will kill or seriously injure me. Each one fears the worst.

Down I go. Round and round I spin like a Catherine wheel. My eyes are open and again I try to grab my ice axe. Futile. My eyes are closed and bump, bump, bump over rocks I go. Then thump and stillness.

I know I'm lying on my front. My shoulder hurts and my neck aches and my eyes are shut but I don't know if I'm alive or dead. I wonder what I'll see when I open my eyes. Will it be the darkness of death or a scene of hell or a scene of heaven whatever they might be?

I open my eyes and look. What joy! It is the world of mountains and rocks. I am alive in my own world. My neck and shoulder hurt but when I move my other limbs slightly there is no pain. "How amazing," I think.

I was lucky to be alive but I was miraculously fortunate to be so uninjured, so unscathed from what was about a three hundred metre (1,000 foot) fall.

I lay on my front for some time, relishing my survival, when I heard Titch's voice.

"Hey up, Ange. What have you done? Are you hurt?"

As usual Titch had been ahead of us all. Having discovered the gully that we were approaching would be difficult to descend, he was returning to warn us to look for another route down. On his way up he'd heard someone groaning and that was apparently me.

"I've a pain in my neck and shoulder, Titch, but otherwise I seem all right. I'm lucky to be alive."

"Here have this liquorice Panda bar," Titch said and the mint-flavoured liquorice, melted in my mouth, tasting delicious.

Chris Drinkwater arrived next and he and Titch exchanged a few words.

"Come on, Ange. You'd better try and sit up," Chris said.

Stiffly I moved my legs and pushed up on my hands so that I could sit up and lean against the rock barrier, which it would seem had stopped my slide. Chris put a spare down jacket around my shoulders and was explaining how he had imagined he'd find me dead or horribly injured, when Andrew, Roly and Colin arrived.

"Thank God, you're all right," I heard Andrew say. "I blame myself for encouraging you to move more quickly."

Once Roly, as medical officer, had checked me out the fellas began to discuss how to get me down without having to ascend again. Titch and Andrew investigated the gully below where I'd come to my abrupt halt and concluded it could be used to reach the glacier floor. They set up a fixed line from where I sat to the top of the gully. Colin lowered me on a belay of four stacked pegs to Andrew with Chris walking alongside me in support. Then Andrew lowered me over the icy gully rock to Titch standing on the glacier below. Chris followed and together the three of us began to wander across the glacier field in search of the tents. On and on we walked with no sign of the tents. Some of the time I rested on Chris and Titch's arms unwittingly making it more difficult for them to walk. Then Chris went off in one direction, Titch in another and I wandered between them. "Would these fucking tents never appear?" I thought in total exasperation.

And then. There they were. Three sunshine yellow Bibler tents on the glacier at night. It was past eleven p.m.

Roly came and instructed me to have a cup of tea, a painkiller and a wee. An exhausted Colin arrived a little later. I said I hoped I'd see him in the morning. I couldn't help wondering if death would get me yet. Would I have a brain haemorrhage and die in the middle of the night?

So as Colin slept – I tossed and turned the whole night through trying to find a comfortable position with my aching neck and shoulder pains.

The sixteenth of May 2001. What a day!

I had ascended a previously unclimbed Himalayan mountain and lived to tell the tale.

CHAPTER 19

The 'Let's Fucking Get Out Of Here!' Option

I stared at Colin sleeping his deep, deep sleep of the just and found it hard to repress feelings of irritation and envy that, I too, wasn't getting the rest, I so desperately craved. It was six in the morning and I was busting for a wee but felt too lazy to move.

At eight fifteen Colin eventually stirred and asked me how I was.

"I didn't sleep too well. Perhaps I should have taken something for the pain as Roly suggested."

Outside it was snowing heavily. Feeling very lethargic and slow, I took a couple of paracetamols and watched Colin start setting up the stove for a brew. A little later on he encouraged me to get my boots on and go for a stroll to the boulder loo. It was important to get the body moving and to assess my mobility.

The snow fell heavily throughout the morning. We could hear avalanches crashing down all about us and above their crashes Andrew, cursing the avalanches and his trials with the misbehaving hanging stove.

"Oh, my God. There goes another one. Fucking hell. This bloody stove's gone out again."

I was worried about the avalanches too. I had survived the fall. I didn't want to get killed in an avalanche before getting home. Colin blithely remarked as we lay there listening, "We're okay. We're in this nice little Bibler with lots of airspace. No need to worry." But I did.

Chatting about the fall during the course of the morning, I explained how Brian had said it was foolhardy and full of risk to go on an expedition like ours. I'd been concerned that he would be proved correct and it looked like he nearly had been.

"Yes, " Colin said. "There's ~~no doubt expeditions~~ are risky. What we need to do now though, is to get you back to Base Camp and decide how to clear the camps."

We had a meeting in our tent with Titch and Andrew representing Roly and Chris.

"There are two options that I see," Colin opened. "One we transfer some stuff down to Advanced Base Camp and then come back to Camp 2. The second is that we completely clear Camp 2, the stash at Camp 1 and Lakeside and take everything to Advanced Base Camp. What do you think? It'll mean heavy loads."

Everyone sat there thinking a moment until Titch looked around and said, "Well, I don't know about you others but my feeling is – let's get the fucking hell out of here." We all burst out laughing as we recognised this expressed exactly what everybody was feeling. We'd had enough. We'd completed our task. The crashing avalanches, the snow and the mist – we wanted out of it. There was a unanimous vote for the 'let's fucking get out of here' option.

Colin then raised the topic of getting me back to Base Camp as soon possible in case of complications connected with the fall. I would need an escort to carry my gear. Who did I want to choose to go with me?

This question completely threw me. No way did I want to pick out one of my five companions. Any of them would be fine. Titch suggested I might like Chris to accompany me but I replied, "No, I feel I've been landed on Chris a few times and I'm not sure it'd be fair. Why don't we draw straws?"

In the end it was names out of a hat. Titch quickly wrote five sets of initials on small scraps of paper, screwed them up, tossed them into Andrew's cap and shook them about. In went my hand and pulled one out. Slowly unscrewing it and focussing my eyes on the scribble I deciphered the initials: "A. P."

Andrew stared, looking visibly knocked for six and I felt momentarily confused. "How funny it should be Andrew," I thought when our relationship struck me as being the most complicated in some strange way. I wondered how he felt about being landed with me.

"Oh, God," he said, looking around at everyone, "It's me. Oh, God. I'm feeling very dehydrated. I'll have to get some fluid in me and I've had no lunch. Oh, my God. What time should we leave?"

After some chat about what preparations were required it was decided that Andrew and I should leave at one thirty with the aim of reaching Advanced Base Camp before nightfall. We all needed to have lunch and melt snow for a brew and our water bottles. I also had to sort out a light load I could carry and gear for Andrew to carry for me. Titch and Andrew returned to their tents to explain to Roly and Chris what had been decided and to begin their own preparations for departure. It was still snowing steadily and visibility was extremely poor.

As Colin and I worked together sorting out the food and brew we chatted about this and that. I wondered how fast I would be able to walk, conscious that I was moving around the tent in a very stiff and ponderous fashion.

"Oh, you might be slow to start with but you'll quicken up," Colin said reassuringly.

At twenty past one Andrew shouted across that he wasn't quite sorted.

"Give us twenty minutes, Ange, will you?" he called.

Then there was a heavy shower of snow and there was another fifteen minutes delay. I could hear Andrew moaning and mumbling about how difficult it was to cram all my gear into his sack so I called across to him, "Andrew, I can carry something." By two fifteen we were ready to set off into the shroud of mist, which now enveloped the glacier.

"Got to stop for a crap on the way," Andrew muttered distractedly, feeling sick and nauseous with the sense of responsibility for getting me back safely. Thick snow and mist made conditions appalling as we tentatively crossed the glacier like the blind. I hated it. Again I thought, "I've survived my fall. I want to get back home alive. Please let this happen."

There'd been the suggestion that I might need extra support descending the ice field to Camp 1 after my dramatic fall down the mountain but I felt calm and collected about the slopes. I was less happy with the poor visibility and the knowledge that there were crevasses to the left of the icefall. Happily, as we descended the mist cleared slightly and both Andrew and I felt more confident. Puffing and panting occasionally under his heavy load Andrew led me to the stash at Camp 1, which looked completely transformed under the new snow. After a little indecision we left Andrew's spare crampons and a packet of the despised mustard sauce there and didn't pick up the bivvy sack. The others would carry it down for us. Would this be a decision to lament later?

On we went down the icy slopes and on towards the Lakeside site. My pace was slow but I kept going, feeling relieved to return to the Siruanch glacier. We had a wee stop and then set off again into the mist. It must have been at this point that we became disorientated and lost our way. Unfortunately this wasn't fully appreciated until we started ascending more ice slopes. Andrew now stopped dead in his tracks.

"This can't be right," he exclaimed. "It's as if we're going up the slopes of South Lampak."

We decided that we were too far left and started crossing to the right of the glacier, checking with the compass that our direction was north.

"Why don't we use your altimeter as well?" I suggested.

"Watch out for crevasses here," Andrew cautioned just before he sunk into a hole to his thigh. "I hope this isn't a crevasse," he began to say, then, "Good God, it is!" and wriggled out as quick as a flash.

"Oh, no! Not again!" I thought. "I'm going to survive the fall and die in a crevasse!"

And so nervously we trudged on and on and on in the mist.

"Sorry about this, Ange. But the visibility is so poor."

"It's absolutely terrible," I said. "It's not at all easy." And I wondered as darkness fell and we were still wandering like lost souls in purgatory, whether we would end up sleeping in the open that night. Ungrateful thoughts began to creep into my mind. "I wish I'd ask Colin to lead me to Advanced Base Camp. Maybe he wouldn't have had this problem. I'm tired. Will we ever find these bloody tents?"

But to Andrew when he asked how I was, I'd say, "I'm okay, Andrew. A bit tired but I'm all right."

Then all of a sudden Andrew shouted, "Look! These are our old tracks covered by snow."

I looked but could make out nothing. We carried on and he exclaimed again.

"Yes! I remember that particular footstep. I can remember making it." To me this sounded extraordinary and inwardly I remained sceptical but I said, "How far do you think it might be now then?"

"I'm almost positive we're on the right track. Shouldn't be much further than half an hour now."

We trudged on, checking on the altimeter that our height was decreasing and talking a little about my fall. Andrew said that he felt guilty because he'd encouraged me to go fast.

"How do you feel about it now, Ange?" he asked. "It could almost be a Readers' Digest story." And as we floundered our way through the greyness, over the treacherous moraine I began to imagine writing something about my adventure.

Then in the distance came the faint but familiar sound of water trickling down the glacier's wall and my heart at last started to believe that we might find Advanced Base Camp before morning. A short while later like magic the outline of three domed canvases loomed up in front of us.

"Here they are!" Andrew crowed triumphantly; and momentarily stunned and then overwhelmed with relief and joy I cried, "You wonderful person!" and gave him a big hug and a kiss on the cheek. We were back to relative safety.

Masala peanuts, sweeties and water were quick and easy to scoff for supper. We were too exhausted to make a brew. I thought and hoped that the others would arrive the same night but Andrew guessed that they had followed our wandering footsteps and got lost, too.

Colin, Titch, Chris and Roly had dismantled Camp 2 after Andrew and I had disappeared into the mist and ended up carrying the heaviest loads any of them could remember. The descent was a cruel and torrid trial through exceedingly soft, fresh snow, which no one could avoid plunging through to thigh level time and time again. Once on the glacier, in darkness and mist, the foursome had tracked the fresh footsteps Andrew and I had made until they realised that we'd got lost on our way down.

By nine p.m. the four accepted that they couldn't make Advanced Base Camp that night, pitched the Biblers and over a reviving brew and hot soup asked the anxious question, "Have Andrew and Ange found Advanced Base Camp?"

Next morning the four of them were staggering down the glacier, weighed down by their enormous loads, when they suddenly spotted in the distance the Advanced Base Camp marker pole with our red Tirsuli North Wall banner flying. Then they knew, to their great relief, that we'd made the camp without any mishap. Some hours later they were astonished to meet Andrew insouciantly strolling back up the now clear and sunny glacier, swinging a red plastic carrier bag.

At the glacier snout Andrew and I had been thrilled to catch sight of a faraway figure. It was our Base Camp manager, Ranjit, who feeling concerned for our safety had come to look out for us. Ranjit took Andrew's rucksack and accompanied me back to Base Camp while Andrew returned to Advanced Base Camp to collect another load.

That Friday evening, finally reunited in the Base Camp mess tent, adorned with balloons and streamers, we feasted and toasted our successful first ascent and safe return, with the first batch of beer brewed on the Siruanch glacier – Chris Smart's Special.

CHAPTER 20
Shambhu Ka Qilla

It was 1.04 a.m. when I snuggled down into my sleeping bag expecting to have a deep and undisturbed sleep after our triumphant return from the jaws of disaster.

Fifty minutes later I was sat bolt upright sweating with terror. There was a rustling in my tent. I felt for my torch but dare not light it for fear of being frightened to death by what it revealed – a yellow-toothed slavering wicked eyed rat perhaps. Cowering to the side of the tent I opened the inner doors with trembling hands, struggled to undo the outer doors and then dived out gasping for breath. Panic! Panic! Let what ever was in there get out!

I eventually switched on the torch and peered into the tent. There was my store of special treats – a packet of cashew nuts and sweets – with the corners chewed away by a rodent's teeth.

Some time later after hanging the goodies outside in a bag and nervously shaking through the clothes and sleeping bag this intrepid first ascensionist fell into a troubled sleep.

* * *

Saturday the nineeenth of May. I opened my eyes at 7.25 and the sun was shining. Kalu had brought bed tea to our tents and I explained to my next-door neighbour, Titch, the traumas of the night.

"I nearly called to you for help, Titch,." I said.

"Good job you didn't, Ange, you'd never have woken me."

Titch went off to the loo tent and on his way back called out, "Squeak! Squeak! Squeak! Little mouse coming."

"Big mouse!" I shouted back laughing.

But it was no joke really. That mouse ruined my sleep for the next three nights. Having banished it from my inner compartment it used the space between the inner and the outer as a running track and I watched in horror as its magnified shadow scuttled up and down ruining any chance of deep, refreshing sleep. A malignant Mickey Mouse.

A little later I wandered across the camping ground for breakfast in the mess tent. There was no seat so I went to move the beer barrel to sit on it.

"Don't touch that!" everyone shouted at me. (They didn't want me disturbing the sediment.) But feeling fragile after my wretched night I retorted with vehemence, "Well, you could have seen there wasn't a bloody seat for me!"

Colin, recognising the anger in my voice, apologised saying, "Don't take it to heart, Ange," and my ruffled feathers smoothed a little, I sat down to a delicious breakfast over which the conversation turned to clearing Advanced Base Camp.

"So, when shall we go and get the loads?" Andrew asked, as he helped himself to a slice of potato omelette.

"Well, I think everyone's bodies are tired for today," Colin answered. "Thank God," I thought. The idea of going back up the glacier that day was killing. Part of me wondered whether I would visit the glacier again and Roly obviously wondered about this, too.

"We're not expecting Ange to bring down a load, are we?" Roly said.

"Well, I don't know," replied Colin, "she might like to."

"I might like to. I might like to," I thought. "Yes, there was some truth in that. I did want to contribute to this last important expedition task although I didn't look forward to the slog. Groan. I thought I'd seen the glacier for the last time."

The rest of the morning was spent on domestic tasks and a photo shoot. I had a thorough mouse hunt in my tent and then my thoughts returned to the idea of writing a book about the expedition.

"What is the expedition book etiquette?" I wondered, thinking of the various expedition books that I had read. "Do you ask people's permission to write about them?" I decided to find out at lunchtime and began noting down possible chapter headings in my journal.

I was so absorbed in this that I was a little late for lunch but I noticed as I entered the tent that a seat was all ready for me this time and smiled as I sat down. It was while we were dishing out the pea and potato curry that I directed my question to Colin, "What's the etiquette about writing books about expeditions, Colin? I'm thinking I might write one."

"There's none in particular that I know of," Colin replied looking at me curiously.

My comment provoked a bit of a stir. Chris Smart asked if I would change people's names and who would be the male lead. The latter question annoyed me slightly.

"Well, I don't envisage there being one hero as such. We've been working as a team after all but events will be seen and interpreted through my eyes."

"You won't forget to mention I gave you that Panda bar, will you?" Titch enquired mischievously.

"And I gave you a drink of water and Chris his down jacket," Andrew added with a grin.

"What's more important is Chris supplied you with gloves," Colin mentioned. Yes, Chris Drinkwater's ample supply of sky blue woollen gloves had prevented me suffering more than two small patches of frostbite on my fingertips.

The conversation now turned to the journey back to Malari.

"I've been to look at the first section of the route and we'll need a fixed line across the river where the snow bridge was to make it safe for the porters. It can flow quite fast and furious. Who feels like giving me a hand to sort it?" Colin said. There was a loud quiet for palpable seconds, which prompted me to say, "I'll give you a hand, Colin. I've not done it before but I can help."

And so I did, although I was forbidden to go across the river with my bad neck.

By now I had become fairly confident that I wasn't going to suddenly drop down dead as a result of my fall. The dead skin on my black frost bitten fingers felt like cardboard but was completely painless. My left arm was badly bruised and my neck ached dully but otherwise I was suffering no ill effects. I didn't look forward to the long grind but I didn't feel justified in declining another trip up the glacier. We arranged to leave at six next morning.

***

"Farewell – Siruanch Glacier," I murmured to myself as I turned my back on it for the very last time and started to follow Chris Drinkwater up the steep slope to where you could begin contouring around to the lone tree above the rhododendron forest.

We had cleared Advanced Base Camp and were now on the punishing trail back to Base Camp. Then, to my relief and total delight a short while later, on the agonising trudge upwards two porters suddenly appeared and insisted that they carried our rucksacks. They had arrived for the trek back to Malari next day and been sent up by Ranjit to give us a hand with the loads. Bless him. Off the porters went like rockets with Chris and I doing our best to keep up with them.

The remainder of our last day at Base Camp was spent packing up gear. Carrying a load down from the glacier had taken its toll and my neck, back and shoulders ached badly. I determined to let the porters carry as much of my equipment as I could cram into my post sacks.

Over our last supper at Base Camp that evening Colin explained that he had been poring over maps with Momoraj all day trying to determine the position of the mountain that we had climbed, in relation to Chalab. The trouble was none of the maps agreed on Chalab's location. Notwithstanding Momoraj had suggested a Hindi name we could give our previously unclimbed peak, which would recognise its close ties with the three mountains forming the trident of Shiva – Tirsuli, Tirsuli West and Hardeol. This name was Shambhu Ka Qilla and means the fortress of Shiva.

Supper came to an end. We bid each other good night and returned to our tents. As I wandered across the dark camping ground I marvelled to myself. "I, Angela Benham, have made a first ascent of a mountain and we have named it – Shambhu Ka Qilla." I was savouring the sound of Shambhu Ka Qilla as I knelt down to unzip my tent when …zoom! The bloody mouse ran out over my legs!

CHAPTER 21
"Are you all in one piece?"

How beautiful the rhododendron bushes were now with their abundant mauve, lilac and white blossoms glistening in the sunlight and the distorted shapes of the silver birches no longer loomed like evil harpies threatening to tear my eyes out but formed elegant argentine sculptures. Ambling our way down the Siruanch valley the song of redstarts and pipits rang out in the clear spring air amidst the flitterings and flutterings of yellow and black spotted butterflies. It felt wonderful to be alive.

We had said goodbye to Base Camp with a ritual closing down of the toilet tent that had involved the scattering of lime and the throwing on of stones. (Apparently the hole had in former days been a grain store!) Our final task was to make a funeral pyre of all combustible rubbish and pack anything that wouldn't burn for disposal in Delhi. It was essential that we left the camping ground as untainted by our presence as possible.

One by one the porters had loaded themselves up with all the expedition paraphernalia and set off along the track above the deep river gorge. Initially I walked behind a very young Garhwalese lad who tottered dangerously when negotiating the bad step that Colin and I had sought to make safe earlier, but after that he picked up speed. Titch, Roly and Andrew charged on ahead, too, and I found myself loitering and indulging in nature worship and photo opportunities with Colin, the two Chrises and Momoraj.

Past Camp Precarious we went and on to the spot where we had caught our first glimpse of the North Wall of Tirsuli West in all its awesome magnificence. The mountain deigned not to favour us with a final farewell as we ate our lunchtime snack but stubbornly remained veiled in cloud.

We left the land of the mountains with a last hard stare at the Surans Ka Dhura pass now completely clear of snow, let alone life threatening cornices. I followed Momoraj down the steep sided, fiercely angled moraine-filled gully towards Point Eight for many a tedious, ankle-twisting minute, recalling my definition of hell, until at last I spotted a figure sitting on the rocks below waiting for us. Nearer and nearer we clattered and scrambled. Now I could make out it was the porters' agent, Kundan Singh, in his luminescent jacket.

"Hello, Kundan Singh!" I called.

"Are you all right, Angela?" he asked me gravely as I approached, giving my hand a firm shake.

"Oh, yes, yes. I'm fine." I replied with some embarrassment, realising he was referring to my fall, "Just a sore neck."

"God has looked after you," came the solemn response, which embarrassed me even more.

We set off along the Girthi Ganga's shore to a loose scree slope above the river that cut us off from where the jeeps were parked. Momoraj stepped up onto the scree, swayed precariously for a few seconds, steadied himself and was secure. I followed less confidently and instantly began scrabbling for a sound footing.

"Uh-oh, I don't like this," I thought, hearing the turbulent waters of the Girthi thundering hungrily beneath me.

Kundan Singh saw my predicament and, having gained the upper path by a different route, bent down to offer his hand to haul me up. For a few nasty moments we rocked back and forth unsteadily like two well-matched Sumo wrestlers, with stones and pebbles spitting out from under my boots.

Then relief – I was on the top path – and marvelling at God's mysterious ways I walked on to where Titch, Roly,

Andrew and Norbu were relaxing by the jeeps.

"Watcha, boys! Been here long?" I said.

It wasn't just me. One of my post office sacks also escaped a watery grave. It fell off the top of the jeep but fortunately dropped onto the road and didn't roll off the track into the gushing Girthi below. I counted my blessings once again as we resumed the bumpy ride into a totally transformed Malari.

The former ghost town was buzzing with activity and people now. Horses and donkeys, cows and jeeps thronged the street. Women passed each other weighed down with loads of dung and hay. Young men stood around arguing money matters while old men herded goats. Children playing by the water pipe stared as we passed. Mums washing pots and pans in the river looked up with vague interest.

The area where our tents had previously been pitched was now covered with bits of straw and cow dung so we were camped nearer the road with strict instructions to keep our gear hidden under canvas. Meals could be served on our little veranda but not before the sexually suggestive graffiti were removed by a discomforted Ranjit. Yes, Malari had certainly come to life.

That afternoon I spent relaxing in the tent with Frankie Goes To Hollywood's 'The Power of Love' blasting down my lug-holes. Ah, yes – the power of love. It was the homestretch now.

I felt tired and weary but more relaxed as I walked across to the veranda for the evening meal. Colin, Chris Smart and Titch were sitting there with a tall, sharp-featured, young military man with a thin moustache stood by their side addressing them. Official business, eh?

"Good evening," I said with a smile and having shaken the proffered hand took my pew.

The immaculately uniformed Second Lieutenant speaking precise English in a clipped tone launched into his speech.

"My scouts have informed me of your presence here in Malari," he began. I noticed two rough and dusty looking soldiers watching the scenario from the road. "I did not know about you. But it is possible my regiment was away at its celebrations when you arrived." He paused and smiled tightly. Colin offered him a seat.

Down he sat and exquisitely polite conversation was exchanged about his hometown, Lucknow, Colin and Chris' trips in India and his mission in Pakistan. "Kashmir will be lovely again," he oozed dryly. Roly, Chris Drinkwater and Andrew had arrived at the table by now and we were all sitting around the table wondering where things were leading when a jeep drove up, stopped, turned around and disappeared again in the direction of the village. Feet shuffled. Norbu had just suggested tea should be served when the sound of an engine was heard again. A jeep screeched to a halt and Kundan Singh, Raju, Momoraj and several other men piled out of it. With his hair in some disarray Momoraj strode quickly across to the table and greeted our visitor who had stood to receive him.

A business-like exchange followed in which Momoraj explained with some aplomb that he had visited the Lieutenant's barracks when he had been absent and completed the required formalities regarding our expedition. There was an instance of awkwardness as the tall, taut Lieutenant faced the short man from Manipur (sporting a neckerchief at a jaunty angle) and then it passed. The Second Lieutenant (whose father was a Colonel) declined the offers of tea and cane swinging bid us goodbye, climbed into his jeep and returned to his lonely outpost up the hill. Meanwhile a flush-faced Momoraj explained that he had been enjoying a big plate of mutton and chang wine with the villagers when news arrived that the army had come a-visiting. Having fulfilled his duties and obligations to the expedition Momoraj was letting his hair down. Who wanted to join him for a drink after dinner?

My first response was to say no – I felt too tired – but on reflection I decided that this was an opportunity not to be missed. A night on the town in Malari had to be interesting. So having eaten dinner, lubricated with two litres of chang, Momoraj, Ranjit, Raju, Chris Drinkwater, Andrew and I squeezed into a jeep and were whisked downtown. To my astonishment the first venue was too congested so we were led through narrow, winding passageways in between ramshackle wooden houses to a small, dark and dingy room with an earthen floor and dusty carpets arranged around a low earthen table. Raju motioned us to make ourselves comfortable on the rugs and after a quick consultation with Momoraj it seemed that an order was placed with the two village women we had passed as we entered the room. Although I initially hesitated about eating meat, because for many years I'd only eaten fish, when the little dishes of gristly lamb morsels and gravy appeared it seemed rude to refuse them. They were in fact very tasty, if chewy, and slipped down extremely satisfactorily with a swig of chang wine. I was tired and said little but followed with interest the ebb and flow of the conversation as it touched on the origins of Buddhism and food taboos. Momoraj's philosophy was that God had given us three types of teeth so we were made to eat all kinds of food. He'd eaten water buffalo. Raju returned and more food and drink was ordered. Full of red rice, vegetables and chang it was now time to go and stumble back in the dark to the campsite. Seeing me clout my head on the doorway as we left the little house Ranjit obviously decided that I needed taking in hand and gripping my arm firmly steered me along the road. We had one torch between us, which made crossing the river by jumping from rock to rock that little bit more exciting. Like a giggling bunch of adolescents we staggered into the camp and collapsed into our tents. Roly was sound asleep.

***

I saw little of the dramatic journey from Malari to Joshimath next day because I spent much of the time with my head down feeling awful. I blamed it on my aching neck and forgetting to take any travel sickness pills but the others smiled knowingly, callously exhorting me to enjoy the gorgeous gorge scenery. At long last the jeep stopped its torturous twisting and turning and pulled up outside the Dronagiri Hotel. A cold tin of Fanta revived me enough to consider going in search of a telephone. Hello civilisation.

The phone kept ringing and I wondered whether anyone was going to answer it. It was seven o'clock in the morning in Leicester – surely Brian was about to wake the kids for school. Then the receiver was picked up and dropped and picked up again and a sleepy voice mumbled, "Hello. Who's that?"

"Hello, Brian. It's me," I said grinning to myself at the thought of his surprise. There was a silence and then the sleepy voice repeated quizzically, "Who?"

This was beyond a joke. Who else would be ringing at seven in the morning but the much-missed explorer?

"It's me, Brian. It's Angela."

Another moment's silence and then recognition, realisation and delight ringing in his voice the first words Brian blurted out were, "Are you all in one piece?"

Well, what do you say?

"Of course I am. I'm fine. And how are you and the kids?"

CHAPTER 22
Because...

Masochism – 'the enjoyment of what appears to be painful or tiresome'.

Well, that is the colloquial definition given in the big black Oxford dictionary on my knee. What is it that makes a person indulge in fakir-like activities when they could be at home watching the telly? I read the chapters of my book and recognise that many are concerned with the pain and the strain that I encountered on the expedition, the physical demands of which were much more gruelling than I could ever have imagined. "Hell is never-ending moraine," was my phrase. Did I actually enjoy an expedition, which much of the time was painful, exhausting and scary? Why did I feel compelled to walk on red-hot coals, dally with death and knock on the doors of the underworld?

When I first spoke of joining the expedition my husband Brian expressed the view that I had a 'death wish'. But then all high altitude climbers had a 'death wish' in his opinion. He remembered my both horrified and fascinated recounts of the ghastly fates of climbers in mountaineering books over years of bedtime reading. At the end of Heinrich Harrer's book 'The White Spider', which describes the attempts and successes on the ascent of the North Face of the Eiger, there is a fifteen page list which includes details of death and disaster as well as triumph and victory.

Max Sedlmayer and Karl Mehringer – frozen to death. Edi

Rainer, Willy Angerer, Andreas Hinterstoisser and poor Toni Kurz, so near yet so far from salvation – all killed while retreating down the Face. Bartolo Sandri and Mario Menti – fell near the "Difficult Crack". Uly Wyss and Karlheinz Gonda plunged to their death from the summit ice field. Fritz Kasparek was a member of the team that made the first successful ascent of the Eiger's North Face – but a mountain still got him in the end. He fell to his doom on Salcantay in Peru. So many, many mountaineers have died in the bid to reach and return safely from the summit of an elusive peak – Julie Tullis, Alison Hargreaves, Joe Tasker, Peter Boardman – the list goes on and on and on. These individuals must have been aware at some psychological level that they courted death but that is far from saying that they desired death. I certainly wasn't looking to die. I almost bottled out of the climb because I feared dying. But as I've said before all the expedition team members were very much aware that death was a possibility. Could it be that climbing in some way encourages an individual to confront their mortality and come to accept (albeit reluctantly) that their ultimate death is an unavoidable reality?

I have just returned from a weekend climbing trip on the sea cliffs of Gogarth in North Wales. I led a route, which scared me and had me wondering at one point whether I might retreat with my tail between my legs. My climbing partner and I both knew I could just throw in the towel and turn my back on the challenge of cracking the puzzle but I didn't want to concede defeat to the climb or my fear. Moaning and groaning I dithered about on that ledge for nearly an hour and then I got the correct combination of holds and flowed over the bulge onto a delightful slab of quartz. The previous anguish became a memory. My main feeling was immense pleasure that the fear of falling hadn't got the better of me.

I'm sure that it's been said many times. Mountaineers and players of other high-risk sports are more likely to be affirming their love of life than their wish to throw it away. Their notion of a life worth living just tends to be more extreme perhaps.

"No pain. No gain." is a well-known climbing saying that

echoes the more literary quotation from William Blake, "Without contraries is no progression." A goal achieved without effort and anxiety can be pleasurable but the feelings of exultation and satisfaction and delight are much more intense if it has taken blood, sweat, tears and time to achieve them. If you never experience hell, how can you fully appreciate heaven? Paradoxically the stress and the hardship and the frustrations met during the course of an expedition can contribute to it being a more fulfilling experience – particularly if the team gels, works well together and is sensitive to each other's moods and needs.

The bus journey back to Delhi was long and uncomfortable for everybody but with an aching neck that felt as stiff as a rust-encrusted hinge it was particularly unpleasant. Overnight we stopped at a big white hotel attractively set in the Himalayan foothills and enjoyed our first hot showers and clean bed sheets. The hotel dinner was a feast of soup and lentils and curry and rice and poppadams (crispy spiced bread), rounded off with deliciously sweet, hot 'gulab jumans' (small cakes steeped in syrup). Andrew noticing, amidst the jollity, that I was very quiet, asked, "How are you, Ange?"

"Oh, I'm so tired, Andrew, and my neck aches," I sighed. His answer was a neck massage that warmed my heart.

* * *

At the age of ten or so I often used to lie in my bed unable to get to sleep and while away the time imagining great dramas in which I was the heroine rescuing those in distress. This often involved me, Miss Superwoman, scaling huge ivy-covered buildings engulfed in flames in order to rescue the panic-stricken occupants. I was a fearless climber. Does my love of mountaineering stem from this? Am I trying to prove something to myself or other people? If I am, my conclusion is that for me it's an impossible quest. My nature is such that whatever I achieve I have a tendency to fault because it is not perfectly executed. How ironic that it was Miss Superwoman who ended up being rescued on Shambhu Ka Qilla.

On the fourth of December 2001 I was still alive. I had managed to reach and celebrate my fiftieth birthday. Many people had asked me on my return from the Himalayas whether I would go on another expedition. I remember recounting my adventures to a good Red Rope friend to whom I confided with a wry smile, "Shambhu Ka Qilla wasn't worth dying for." With a grin he replied, "What is?"

"Was it worth getting a sore neck which ached a year later?" I ask myself and the answer to that question is, with only a little hesitation, "Yes."

It is good to know you are alive and not totally straitjacketed by your job and your responsibilities. Working on an adventurous project with six interesting and good-hearted individuals does confirm that you have a functioning brain and an active body. There is no place for boredom. The lengthy discussions concerning numbers of tents, batteries, walkie-talkies and painkillers etcetera provide a focus of attention for nearly a year.

"Climb a mountain and prove to yourself you're really alive …if you don't kill yourself in the process!" could be my slogan.

I want to go on an expedition again because I find the process of planning and organising a major project stimulating and full of challenges. I flourish amidst the feelings of comradeship, resolution, joy and angst that can consume an expedition team. It fills me with dynamism.

But I don't really want to die on a wind swept ridge or at the bottom of an ice-cold crevasse. I am relieved that I did not bump and slide and slither and thump to an early grave at the foot of Shambhu Ka Qilla.

I am lucky to be alive and wish to remain so for many years to come.

However the fear of death won't stop me pursuing more adventures in the High Mountains because in my opinion people don't climb a mountain because it is there; they climb it because they are putting two fingers up to Death.

CHAPTER 23
Postscript

One year later and I'm sitting at my computer reflecting on the remarkable events that have taken place in my life since I walked down the glacier with my scratched nose and poorly neck.

My fantasy has come true.

I've escaped the classroom.

From Christmas 2001 until May 2002 I had a roller-coaster ride of hope and disappointment while Leicester City Education Authority considered whether my application for early retirement from teaching could be accepted. In the end it was the actions of a lone Head Teacher unexpectedly making one of her staff redundant, which released the bolt for me at the eleventh hour and I was granted early retirement.

The shock was almost greater than that after my fall down Shambhu Ka Qilla!

At the end of August I'll be getting on an aeroplane for the Alps instead of picking up my chalk and mortarboard.

* * *

Then you, my reader – sat in your armchair or relaxing on the beach, waiting at a train station or snuggled under your duvet with the bedside clock gently ticking – are reading the book that I began to formulate in my mind as I picked my painful way down the moraine, daring to dream that it might reach the light of day.

For me the wonder and the irony is that I had to nearly die for this book to have the chance of life. The energy to sit down and craft this story comes from the thrill of being spared yet again.

What's more where would a mountaineering yarn be without somebody hurting themselves at least a little bit?

* * *

How much like climbing a mountain – is writing and getting a book published.

You need plenty of stamina and persistence plus the ability to work both day and night. Steadfast friends and family must continue their support despite how boring you become with your one-track mind. Good equipment, a nutritious diet and plenty of fluids are essential but what will have the most influence on whether you reach the top and triumph is – Good Luck.

Angela Benham

ACKNOWLEDGEMENTS

I have read many mountaineering books since my interest in climbing was re-awoken in the early nineteen nineties and I have referred to some in *Lucky To Be Alive*. I would like to acknowledge the impact that this mountaineering literature has had on my writing while at the same time hoping that it is evident that I have a unique style of my own.

Below I acknowledge the specific references I have made to other climbers' books, articles and reports with my thanks for being allowed to use them in *Lucky To Be Alive*.

p. 9 from Croz Solo by Alison Hargreaves, published by High Mountain Sports magazine June 1994

p. 10 from *Dark Shadows Falling* by Joe Simpson, published by Jonathan Cape. Reprinted by permission of The Random House Group Ltd.

p. 11 from "Women, Freedom and Risk" by Ed Douglas, published by *Climber Magazine* June 1998

p. 20 from *The Scottish Himalayan Expedition* by W. H. Murray, published by J. M. Dent & Sons Ltd. 1951

p. 20 from Shambhu Ka Qilla (2001) The Tirsuli North Wall 2001 Group expedition to the Upper Siruanch Glacier Basin report

p. 53 from Independence Peak (1997) The Chandra Bhaga Expedition Group expedition to CB11

Other Books of Interest

From Northern Liberties Press and Old City Publishing

Invisible on Everest: Innovation and the Gear Makers
By Mike Parsons and Mary B. Rose
320 pp + 4pp of color illustrations + 90 b&w illustrations
ISBN 0-9704143-5-8 • Price UK £24.99 • USA $36.00

Lucky to be Alive By Angela Benham
186 pages • 18 color illustrations • ISBN 0-9704143-6-6 • Paper • $14.95 • £9.50

A Price Guide To Books Concerning British Mountaineers and Mountaineering in the British Isles 1781-1999 By Dek Palmer
122 pages + i-viii • ISBN 0-9704143-0-7 • £9.95 • $14.95

A Price Guide to Books Concerning Mountaineering in the Himalayas
By Dek Palmer • 152 pp + i-viii • ISBN 0-9704143-2-3 • £9.95 • $14.95

ORDER FORM

AUTHOR/TITLE	ISBN	QUANTITY	PRICE

☐ CHECK (payable to Old City Publishing)
☐ CREDIT CARD ☐ CASH ☐ BILL

CREDIT CARD INFORMATION
☐ MASTERCARD ☐ VISA ☐ DISCOVER

ACCOUNT NUMBER

EXPIRATION DATE ☐☐/☐☐

TOTAL

NAME
ADDRESS
CITY STATE ZIP
COUNTRY
TELEPHONE
E-MAIL
SIGNATURE

Old City Publishing
628 North 2nd Street,
Philadelphia, PA 19123
USA
TEL +1 215 925 4390
FAX +1 215 925 4371
e-mail info@oldcitypublishing.com
web www.oldcitypublishing.com

OLD CITY PUBLISHING
NORTHERN LIBERTIES PRESS

Fax orders to: +1 215 925 4371

Other Books of Interest

From Northern Liberties Press and Old City Publishing

INVISIBLE ON EVEREST: INNOVATION AND THE GEAR MAKERS
By Mike Parsons and Mary B. Rose
320 pp + 4 pp of color illustrations + 90 b&w illustrations
ISBN 0-9704143-5-8 • Price: UK £24.99 • USA $36.00

LUCKY TO BE ALIVE By Angela Benham
186 pages • 18 color illustrations • ISBN 0-9704143-6-6 • Paper • $14.95 • £9.50

A PRICE GUIDE TO BOOKS CONCERNING BRITISH MOUNTAINEERS AND MOUNTAINEERING IN THE BRITISH ISLES 1781-1999 By DEK PALMER
122 pages + i-viii • ISBN 0-9704143-0-7 • £9.95 • $14.95

A PRICE GUIDE TO BOOKS CONCERNING MOUNTAINEERING IN THE HIMALAYAS
By DEK PALMER • 152 pp + i-viii • ISBN 0-9704143-2-3 • £9.95 • $14.95

ORDER FORM

AUTHOR/TITLE	ISBN	QUANTITY	PRICE

nlp

OLD CITY PUBLISHING

☐ CHECK (payable to Old City Publishing)
☐ CREDIT CARD ☐ CASH ☐ BILL

CREDIT CARD INFORMATION:

☐ MASTERCARD ☐ VISA ☐ DISCOVER

ACCOUNT NUMBER ______________________

EXPIRATION DATE ☐☐ / ☐☐

TOTAL ______________

NAME ______________________
ADDRESS ______________________
____
CITY ____________ STATE ______ ZIP ____________
COUNTRY ______________________
TELEPHONE ______________________
E-MAIL ______________________

SIGNATURE ______________________

Old City Publishing
628 NORTH 2ND STREET,
PHILADELPHIA, PA 19123
USA
TEL: +1 215 925 4390
FAX: +1 215 925 4371
e-mail: info@oldcitypublishing.com
web: www.oldcitypublishing.com

OLD CITY PUBLISHING
NORTHERN LIBERTIES PRESS
Fax orders to: +1 215 925 4371